what the heck am I going to do with my life?

MARGARET FEINBERG

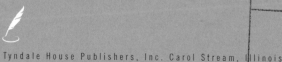

Tyndale House Publishers, Inc. Carol Stream, Illinois

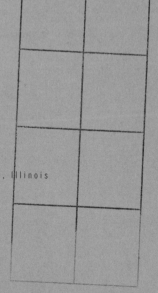

Visit Tyndale's exciting Web site at www.tyndale.com

TYNDALE is a registered trademark of Tyndale House Publishers, Inc.

Tyndale's quill logo is a trademark of Tyndale House Publishers, Inc.

What the Heck Am I Going to Do with My Life?

Designed by Luke Daab

Edited by Sarah Mason

Unless otherwise indicated, all Scripture quotations are taken from the *Holy Bible,* New International Version® NIV®. Copyright © 1973, 1978, 1984 by International Bible Society. Used by permission of Zondervan. All rights reserved.

Scripture quotations marked NLT are taken from the *Holy Bible,* New Living Translation, copyright © 1996, 2004. Used by permission of Tyndale House Publishers, Inc., Carol Stream, Illinois 60188. All rights reserved.

Scripture marked "The Message" taken from *THE MESSAGE.* Copyright © 1993, 1994, 1995, 1996, 2000, 2001, 2002. Used by permission of NavPress Publishing Group.

Library of Congress Cataloging-in-Publication Data

Feinberg, Margaret, date.
    What the heck am I going to do with my life? / Margaret Feinberg.
       p. cm.
    Includes bibliographical references (p.   ) .
    ISBN-13: 978-1-4143-0557-8 (sc : alk. paper)
    ISBN-10: 1-4143-0557-5 (sc : alk. paper)
    1. Vocation—Christianity.   2. Young adults—Religious life. I. Title.
    BV4740.F45 2005
    248.4—dc22   2005023225

Printed in the United States of America

12   11   10   09   08   07   06
7   6   5   4   3   2

To every person who has ever desired to live outside the box and had the guts to do it. I stand in awe of your courage, creativity, and raw talent. You are my heroes.

Contents

Acknowledgments

Thank you to Jerry Slocum, Anne Abernathy, Dois I. Rosser Jr., Dwight "Ike" Reighard, Ken Frantz, Os Hillman, Brian Mosley, and Betsy Taylor for all of your wisdom and insight. Thank you to my husband and editor extraordinaire (is that how you spell that, honey?). A special thank you to Corrine Ferguson for taking way too many tests and quizzes. And many thanks to Robert and Andrea Jobe for your prayers. You know how to mess up a good book and make it better. Thank you to Mariam Kamell for all your help and support—especially with understanding calling and destiny. Thank you to Sarah Mason for your sagelike wisdom in editing. And a big Alaskan hug to Ken Petersen for going above and beyond to breathe life and depth into this project.

What the heck am I going to do with my life? It is a question that just won't go away. You probably remember being asked as a child, *What do you want to do when you grow up?* You may have listed one of the more popular answers: a schoolteacher, doctor, lawyer, or fireman. Maybe you dreamed big and wanted to be an astronaut or win a Miss America Pageant. Or maybe you were a little different from the other kids and wanted to be a body-builder, design roller coasters, or serve as an international diplomat to a third-world country. I was one of those "special" kids.

When you finally secured a diploma—whether from high school or college—people rephrased the same basic question: *What are you going to do after graduation?* Unless you wanted to be caught like a deer in the headlights over and over again, you needed an answer, an internship, a part-time job—anything to make the question go away.

Maybe you just graduated with a degree in business only to discover that you hate business. You like the idea of being a teacher except for the students, or you love public service except for the people. The reality hits that you've spent the last few years pursuing a career, and now you wonder if there's something else you should be or want to be doing. You stare down the long road to retirement and quietly wonder, *Now what?* You can't help but think that you really should have all this figured out by now. You keep asking yourself the familiar question, *What the heck am I going to do with my life?*

You are not alone.

It is a question we all ask ourselves from time to time, usually more often than we want to admit. Even when the question disappears for a while, it usually makes a reappearance in a different stage of life. Just when you think you have the answer, something happens, circumstances change, and you are left wondering, *What the heck am I going to do now?*

As a child, Darlene wanted to be a waitress like her mother. Darlene began working at Denny's at the age of fourteen and dreamed about being a veterinarian one day. But by the time she enrolled in Adams State College, she had no idea what she wanted to do. For the first two years she explored her options. She studied music because she liked to sing, then shifted to music education because she liked kids, too. When she discovered she didn't want to teach music theory, she switched to an elementary education major, but a semester into the classes she changed to psychology. Then she took a Spanish class and got hooked on learning a foreign language. She plans to graduate with two majors: psychology and Spanish.

Now twenty-two, Darlene concludes, "I have absolutely no idea what I want to do with my life. I am at that funny transition period now where I should be making decisions and choices. The doors of possibilities are all open and I am overwhelmed. All I know is that I will be happy to return home and start working at Denny's again until I figure out the next step."

Everyone has Denny's Moments—the desire to return to a place that's safe and comfortable and will allow us to figure out who we are and what we're going to do. My own Denny's

Thinking of taking some time off to discover your passion or just find yourself?
If so, here are a few ideas:

Seasonal Work. Whether you work in a ski lodge or as a lifeguard, most towns with a tourist industry desperately need seasonal workers. Can you drive a van, clean a room, or check in a hotel guest? The jobs may not be glamorous, but they'll buy you time to relax and reflect.

Temp Agency. Sure, you might get offered some pretty odd jobs—one guy I know was hired to sit by the highway and record the number of cars that went by—but the great thing with a temp agency is that you can always say no if the job doesn't suit your fancy (or you don't own a suit). With temp jobs, you can agree to your own hours and expose yourself to new professions and work environments along the way.

Move Back In with Mom and Dad. Probably one of the least popular options, but it's becoming more common than you can imagine. In fact, 60 percent of college grads now estimate that they'll be heading back home after diploma day. So if your old room is still available and the 'rents are willing to taking you back, enjoy the opportunity for downtime.

Caretaking. These gigs can be hard to get, but there's nothing like living rent free and even getting paid for a little maintenance. Let people know you're interested in caretaking. Put an ad in the paper. Advertise online. You never know when the owner of a phat pad just might need you.

Moments have taken many forms—ski instructor, nanny, caterer, housekeeper, and all kinds of part-time jobs that bought me enough time to figure out what was next. Maybe you are in a Denny's Moment right now, or maybe you know deep down inside that it is time to take a step back from your current job and exhale.

Wherever you are in life, this book is designed as a reminder that everyone wrestles with questions of calling, vocation, risk, and courage in one form or another. *Can I really do it? Is it worth it? Where do I begin?* These are the questions that make us human, and they're more relevant today than ever.

Whether you realize it or not, a dramatic change has occurred in the workplace over the last twenty to thirty years. For previous generations, a job was just that—a job. You put in your hours and earned your pay. A good job was a good-*paying* job. But as the pace of life and length of the work-week have continued to increase, more and more people look to their workplaces to provide more than just a paycheck. Today's dream job provides meaning, purpose, and authentic community. It fosters personal growth, develops individual talents, and allows you to make our planet a little better at the end of the day. And, oh yeah, it allows you to pay back all those student loans (ahead of schedule) and afford a few urban sprees or at least a really nice vacation on a tropical beach with friends. In other words, a job title twenty years ago was a reflection of what you did. A job title today is a reflection of who you are.

That's why, in the following pages, you'll be challenged to

answer tough questions about what motivates you, what stops you from taking bigger risks, and how you can do a better job of balancing your life, career, and faith. You'll be asked questions not just about what you do, but about who you are and who you're called to be.

The quizzes, tests, and spaces to journal and even draw add an interactive element that will challenge you to reflect on your unique personality, talents, and rhythms.[1] The chapters are filled with the journeys of everyday people, like you and me, who have asked the same pivotal question and struggled to find an answer. To gather these stories, I took a few risks of my own by calling, e-mailing, and interviewing more than a handful of individuals, including personal heroes. The topics explored in the chapters—direction, calling, passion, reality, and impact, among others—stand alone as their own entities. They raise questions, explore principles, and uncover truths.

While this book will serve as a helpful guide for your personal journey, you won't be able to open to page 73 and discover that you really were meant to be a police officer or flip to page 94 and realize that it is time to call it quits on that dream of being a rock star. You won't find five easy steps, six quick methods, or seven fast rules in the pages that follow. That would be too easy. Rather, *What the Heck Am I Going to Do with My Life?* is designed to take you on a journey of discovery. By the time you finish this book, you still may not have a fill-in-the-blanks response to *What the heck am I going to do with my life?* but maybe—just maybe—you'll be one step closer to discovering the answer for yourself.

Resolve Career Distress

Feeling a little distressed rather than de-stressed when it comes to your career? If so, you're not alone. How do you overcome all the obstacles to resolving career distress? Barbara Moses, PhD, author of *What Next? The Complete Guide to Taking Control of Your Working Life*, advises

Focus on the real issues. Don't use global language like "I hate this job." Be specific about what you don't like. Sometimes just articulating a specific issue brings insight for a solution that may actually be a minor adjustment rather than a cataclysmic change.

Acknowledge that you have a problem.
It doesn't make you weaker. Indeed, it takes a strong and optimistic person to say, "I am unhappy. I deserve more. I am prepared to identify what I need to do to be happier."

Don't expect a magic-button solution. Be prepared to live with uncertainty and confusion while you dig through the issues and possibilities. It takes time to envision what's next.

Make a plan. It can take a couple of years if you need to get your finances in order, upgrade your education, or develop a network of contacts in a future field.

Identify what's holding you back. Is it fear of failure? a lack of clear vision? loyalty to others? insufficient confidence in yourself? Whatever it is, face up to it! Write it down or say it out loud. Think about whether your fears and anxieties are realistic. Everyone has these fears. They don't make you foolish.

Give yourself permission to dream. Often people feel silly or self-indulgent when they fantasize about a dream job. But it can actually provide important clues about what you feel you're missing and what you need to feel good about your work, whether at the same job or in moving on.

Don't overestimate the consequences of change. You may fear that your world is going to be turned upside down, but once you develop a plan, you will realize or find ways to ensure that a move will have only a modest impact—and improve your happiness factor.

Get support. One of the most significant contributors to successful transitions is having a group of people you can go to for cheerleading. Friends and family can provide important emotional support, but they are not experts on work and cannot see you objectively. In addition, complex psychological issues often underlie career distress. Consult a career counselor who can act as a neutral sounding board and provide structure to help you identify the problem, overcome inertia, work through critical decisions, and develop a realistic course of action. Check the Association of Career Professionals International (www.acpinternational.org) for a listing of consultants by location.*

*Adapted from What Next? The Complete Guide to Taking Control of Your Working Life by Barbara Moses, PhD (New York: DK Publishing, Inc., 2003). Used with permission. For more information on Barbara Moses and BBM Human Resource Consultants, Inc., visit www.bmoses.com/.

Launch:

Where Do We Go from Here?

Forget what's available out there. Go after the job that you really want the most.

David Maister

More adults than I care to remember have asked me about my future plans. Maybe they saw it as an easy way to involve a child in a conversation. Maybe they did it for sport. Maybe they were looking for suggestions for themselves. Whatever the cause, it seemed like I was never too young to know what I wanted to do when I grew up.

By the time I was four, I had decided that I wanted to be Wonder Woman. My mom invested in a hearty pair of Underoos, and I was convinced that I would be a perfect superhero. The real Wonder Woman had to retire someday. Alone in my room, I practiced warding off invisible villains and intruders with my imaginary bulletproof gold bracelets and belt of truth. I kept asking my mom to buy the kids' version of the belt and bracelets, but I must have lost interest or grown out of my Underoos by Christmas because the accessories never arrived.

After battling the forces of darkness, I decided to make a career change. By the age of five, I knew what I really wanted to be when I grew up: a doctor. I had the plastic Fisher-Price Medical Kit to prove it. I learned to use a stethoscope, thermometer, and blood pressure gauge. I made my friends say ahh and checked their temperatures before they were allowed to come over to play.

Medicine seemed destined to be my future until the summer that I spent every waking moment watching the Olympic Games. At the end of two weeks, I knew my calling: I was meant to be a gymnast. I tumbled all over the living room floor and my bed. I ran into tables and walls and over the dog at least three times. A handful of concussions later, I began rethinking my blurry future.

Fortunately, the winter games were only a few months away. I calculated the sport that would give me the best chance at winning a gold medal. After two weeks of Olympic glory, I knew I was created for the biathlon, a combination of cross-country skiing and rifle shooting. The reasoning was truly elementary: If I wasn't a fast skier, I could make up for it by shooting well, and if I couldn't hit the bull's-eye, I could still outski the other racers. I was confident I could become good at one if not both of the required skills. Besides, it wasn't a particularly popular sport, so I knew the overall odds of qualifying and competing were better.

A few months after the closing ceremonies, I could still taste Olympic gold. My father surprised me with a small Browning .22 rifle for my birthday. I was thrilled and I was determined. I knew I had less than four years to become the youngest member of the Olympic biathlon team. My father set up a series of paper targets on the woodpile. Hour after hour, I shot and reloaded. Day after day, I honed my skills. I knew it was a matter of destiny—until I got tired of practicing on day four. Video games and playing in the woods with friends were more fun. I hung my little .22 rifle—along with my Olympic dreams—on the mantel.

> But don't think for a second that I quit dreaming.

As I grew older, I went through countless other vocations. I wanted to study ballet until I discovered what it meant to be on pointe. I wanted to be a pianist until I learned how many hours of practice it required. I wanted to be a musician until I realized I couldn't keep a beat or sing in tune. I wanted to be an astronaut until Mom said no to two very expensive weeks at Space Camp. I wanted to be a lawyer until I learned that sometimes you have to defend the bad guys. I wanted to be a teacher until I discovered what being confined in a room with 18 six-year-olds does to me. I wanted to be a computer programmer until I realized I could never remember the code. And I wanted to be an ambassador to a third-world country until Georgetown University sent me a denied admittance slip.

YOUR CHILDHOOD DREAMS

When you were a child, what did you dream of doing or becoming when you grew up? Make a list of some of your interests below.

Profession/Interest   What attracted you to that profession?

_____   _____

_____   _____

_____   _____

Did you give up on the dream? Why or why not? How do you feel about your choice now?

_____

_____

_____

_____

My parents were always willing to support my whims. My grandfather repeatedly told my mother when she was young, "You could be the first female president of the United States. Nothing is impossible." As a result, I grew up with the same mantra and was eager to believe it. In fact, my high school yearbook has dozens of autographs from fellow students that say, "Good luck in the presidential election in 2020." Whenever I go back and read them, I laugh. The year 2020 isn't as far away anymore.

I basically grew up trying to answer the question, *What the heck am I going to do with my life?* At the time that I needed the answer the most—during college, when you have to declare a major—I had no idea what I wanted to do. Fortunately, something greater than myself was at work. Because of a computer error, I ended up in two religion courses my first semester. I tried to resolve the issue, but by the time I finally reached the level of personnel who could correct the error, the last day to change courses had already passed. I spent a semester taking one rather forgettable religion course and another that changed my life, taught by a man I will never forget.

His name was Dr. Fred Horton. An active Episcopal priest and head of the religion department, Fred Horton surprised me by asking a simple question the first time I stepped into his office: "How are you doing?"

I offered a quick reply and hurried to discuss the coursework matter at hand. In midsentence, he stopped me and asked, "How are you *really* doing?"

I rambled some honest answer about struggling with the transition to college life.

"Well, if you ever want to come back to talk, let me know," he replied.

Over the next four years I accepted his invitation many times. In fact, I ended up majoring in religion, and Dr. Horton became an incredible source of encouragement and a mentor to me. What I once dubbed a scheduling mistake was used by God to help change the course of my life.

The religion major provided a brief hiatus from the impending question, but as graduation approached, *What the heck are you going to do with your life?* became the topic of choice for nearly everyone that my parents and I encountered. It was exhausting.

Job (n. 'jäb): A person meeting a need and getting paid to do it.

Believe it or not, people get paid to

• practice quality control for potato chips and candy bars

• design paintball guns

• work as Brad Pitt's assistant

• film segments for the Discovery Channel

• train dolphins

• make surfboards

• design greeting cards

• take photos of exotic locations

• work behind the scenes for cable-news stations

• create computer games

• make music videos

• lead hunting expeditions

• review movies

• design new toys

Unsure of which direction to go, I sent out applications to anywhere that piqued my interest. I applied to Hebrew University in Israel, graduate school, and an internship at a small religious magazine in Florida. All the doors closed except for the internship—which turned out to be with a sister magazine to the one I had applied for—and I spent a summer sweating it out in Orlando. Afterward, I went on a weeklong mission trip that lasted more than a month and then returned for a second stint, where I discovered the hard way that I simply wasn't missions material.[1]

I came back to the United States nearly a year after I graduated and faced the doomsday question yet again. I was living at home and working as a ski instructor, kids adventure camp counselor, and nanny. I asked myself a different question: *If I could do anything with my life, assuming that time and money were no object, what would I choose to do?*

The answer came almost instantly. From the deepest part of my being, I wanted to write.

Then I had to face the follow-up question: *What is stopping me from doing it?*

At that moment, the insecurities and fears rose to the surface. What if, like mission work, writing didn't work out? What if I couldn't get published? What if I didn't have the discipline? What if I couldn't feed myself doing it? What if I had to live with Mom and Dad forever?

As I bounced between the emotions related to every concern, I realized that my desire to write was greater than any of my fears or insecurities. I went to the library and researched publishing opportunities. I sent off clips to several Christian magazines and asked if I could write small reviews for the backs of their publications. All but one said yes. Over the next five years, I grew from writing reviews to news stories to feature stories to magazine cover stories. In

2002, Relevant Books published my first book, *God Whispers: Learning to Hear His Voice.*

Today, when people ask what the heck I'm going to do with my life, I have my fallback answer: I am going to write. I'm a writer. That's what I do. Yet even with what most people would consider a career, I can't help but wonder if there's something more. I can't help but revisit the basic questions I have been wrestling with since those days when I could still fit into a pair of Underoos: *What am I going to do with my life? What's next? What's around the corner? What more could I be doing? What could I be doing better now?*

I have asked these questions so many times that I am convinced I should have the answers by now. The problem is that just as soon as I develop an answer, something radically changes in my life or I'm introduced to something new, and I'm forced to revisit the questions again.

I know that I am not alone. I have interviewed more than one hundred people of all ages and backgrounds from around the country, and everyone I've spoken with has wrestled with this question in one form or another.

Even those who have known what they wanted to do since they were knee-high to a grasshopper still admit to struggling and second-guessing along the journey.

Those in their twenties and thirties are particularly vulnerable to soul-searching, but they are joined by people of all ages.

Beth, a twenty-five-year-old, says that when she enrolled

in college, she realized it was time to finally answer the question, What do you want to be when you grow up? The only problem was that she didn't have an answer.

"I think I put a lot of pressure on myself feeling that my job would be my life's purpose, so I wanted it to be something I really had a passion for and would enjoy doing," she says. "I took a lot of different classes my first few years of college trying to figure it all out. I envied my roommate and others who just knew from the time they were small and were on their way to doing it. I, on the other hand, would spend much time wondering and praying about what I would do."

In college, Beth took an Introduction to Social Work class and felt that out of everything she studied, the subject matter was the closest she could come to picking a career once she graduated. "Deep down I think I knew that wasn't the best thing, but it was the best thing at the time," she says.

She graduated with a degree in social work and worked in the field for a few years. "I loved the work and the children I worked with and felt like when I went home and laid my head down at night, I had spent the day doing something worthwhile [for] society and purposeful. But I became burned out from working way too many hours in very stressful situations and realized that I could not continue the pace and demands that social work required for the rest of my life."

Beth began to wonder what else she could do with her life. "There I was again, wondering what in the world I wanted to be and do and a bit frustrated to be in that place again. I began fervently praying and seeking God's direction and knew that even though I had no idea, he had formed and made me and knew the answers I was searching for. So I prayed and waited."

In the meantime, she quit her job and moved home with her parents to rest and de-stress for a month. She continued praying and began substitute teaching to pay the bills. "[God] began to put the field of nursing on my heart," she recalls. "I looked into it, and I am now completing my first semester of nursing school. I'm starting over, wondering what in the heck I'm doing in nursing school but feeling a remarkable peace."

Beth says she has come to terms with the fact that life is too complex to figure it all out. "I wish someone had told me when I was in school the first time that it was okay if I didn't know. At that age it is kind of hard to know what you want to do with the rest of your life. I really had to go out into the world and get some life into me before I really could see and know what all is out there to be and do. I think I put way too much pressure on myself and didn't enjoy the process of not knowing and discovering what I liked and might be good at doing."

I can identify all too well with the stress and pressure Beth describes. Figuring out what to do with your life isn't easy because even after landing a job or finally earning a few years' work experience to put on the résumé, the questions about what you are going to do don't always disappear. They just keep resurfacing. Singles, newlyweds, oldlyweds, empty nesters, retirees—anyone at any age or stage in life—can wrestle with these questions and struggle to find answers. No one is immune.

That's one reason I think *What the heck am I going to do with my life?* is one of the greatest questions we will ever ask ourselves. Not just because it is the question that won't go away, but because it forces us to examine ourselves in a new light— who we are today and who we are called to be tomorrow. The question challenges us to look at the core of who we are as individuals, discover our talents and gifts, and come to terms with our weaknesses. When we dare to ask, we step into a realm where anything—including growth, transformation, and change—is possible. Risk, failure, and loss are all potential outcomes, but so are success, innovation, and building a legacy that lives beyond us.

What the heck am I going to do with my life? isn't a safe question, but it has the power to awaken dormant dreams and silent desires. It has the ability to both compel and propel us to fulfill our lifelong calling and purpose. And that makes it a question worth asking.

Looking for Work to Get You through
Till You Know What You Want to Do?
Check out these cool Web sites:

www.coolworks.com

www.groovejob.com

www.hotjobs.com

www.wetfeet.com

www.snagajob.com

www.backdoorjobs.com

.0002

Direction:

What Pushes You?

I can't imagine someone not knowing what to do with their life. I'd say, What's your fantasy? Check with God about it. If God says yes, then chase it down.

Victoria Jackson, former comedian on *Saturday Night Live*

Next to my desk I keep a well-worn manila folder of personal heroes. It is a humble file, but it contains greatness. Most of the people featured in the odd assortment of articles and clippings have never climbed Mount Everest, won an Olympic medal, or landed on the cover of *Entertainment Weekly,* but something about what they do—their tenacity, focus, passion, or insight—resonates deep within my being. Jerry Slocum is one of those people.

I met Jerry in the September/October 2004 issue of *AARP,* a magazine that I really shouldn't be reading for another three or four decades except for the fact that I think it is one of the best-kept secrets in American publishing (it's the official publication of the American Association of Retired Persons). The half-page article revealed that Jerry is one of the world authorities on mechanical puzzles, something I knew little to nothing about. In fact, he has managed to collect more than thirty thousand mechanical puzzles over the course of his life. To enter the library and museum on his Beverly Hills property, you have to solve a puzzle. Where did this seventy-two-year-old develop such a passion for puzzles? I had to know.

So I called him. Through a warm and insightful conversation, I learned that Jerry Slocum has always had an inclination to take things apart. As a child, he faced significant medical challenges. He loved it when one of his parents would give him a clock to dismantle while he was confined to his bed. Jerry remembers his father returning from trips with gifts. Instead of buying the typical cap pistol or spinning top, his father brought him puzzles, which were always challenging and rewarding to solve. At the age of ten, Jerry saved his quarter-a-week allowance to purchase his first puzzle: Chinese rings. He spent several days trying to remove the bar from the series of wire and rings. When he finally solved the puzzle, he felt a rush of satisfaction. Jerry continued buying various types of mechanical puzzles, and by the time he entered high school, he realized he had inadvertently started a collection.

When it came time to enroll in college, Jerry chose the University of Illinois, where he majored in mechanical engineering and minored in psychology—fields that involved problem solving. After graduation, he accepted a job at Hughes Aircraft—founded by Howard Hughes and featured in the film *The Aviator*—where he worked on the design of cockpits for military planes. For the next thirty years, he built countless products that went into airline production and had a major influence on how military cockpits are designed today. Reflecting on his career, he notes that the combination of engineering and psychology applied to everything he did.

"To design cockpits for pilots, I had to understand both engineering and people and their capabilities," he says.

Jerry remained fascinated with puzzles. He used the small devices as an icebreaker for coworkers at Hughes Aircraft. Even after receiving multiple promotions, he was still asked to bring his puzzles on corporate retreats to build camaraderie and strengthen relationships among executives.

In May 1955, Jerry took his hobby one step further when he published an article in *Science and Mechanics* on making and solving puzzles. Soon after, he began receiving letters from people all over the world who didn't think that anyone else collected mechanical puzzles. Jerry kept track of all the letters, and in 1978 he invited his puzzle friends to his home for the first International Puzzle Party. After eight Puzzle Parties, the gathering outgrew his home and became an annual event that now alternates between the United States, Japan, and Europe.

Today Jerry Slocum maintains a private puzzle museum in the two-story building behind his Beverly Hills home. He has organized puzzle exhibitions for museums around the country. In addition, he's penned nearly a dozen books and appeared on shows hosted by Johnny Carson and Martha Stewart.

Even after decades of studying and solving mechanical puzzles, Jerry's interest is as alive as ever. "It is such a thrill to solve them and conquer them," he says. "I think there's a gratification that comes when you try something difficult and solve it."

Jerry notes that—like life—many puzzles don't have clear solutions. They require innovation, creativity, and the willingness to face a challenge. "One of the things you learn through solving puzzles is that you can't look for the obvious solution and keep trying it over and over, because you'll fail," he says. "You have to look at unusual and unorthodox ways of solving the problem. You have to shift to trying to do something one way and then the other, the way the inventor might have. It stimulates your thinking and logic and analysis."

By the time I finished the conversation with Jerry, I felt like I was ready to spend the afternoon trying to solve puzzles. The man has passion. He was able to use a simple fascination with mechanical puzzles to build relationships, enhance his career, learn valuable life lessons, and bring people from all over the world together. His story will remain in my manila folder for years to come.[1]

Yet something about Jerry Slocum still puzzles me (pardon the pun). Where did his passion for mechanical puzzles come from?

Jerry is quick to highlight moments in his childhood when he dissected clocks and discovered different kinds of puzzles, but I wonder if there's something more. Was problem-solving a natural gift for him? Did his parents inadvertently encourage him to pursue mechanical puzzles as a pastime? And how did he manage to keep his fascination alive for so many years?

Jerry's story raises questions about our own stories and what pushes us into pursuing particular careers, interests, hobbies, and pastimes. Sometimes by looking into your past, you can find clues about the direction of your future. There may be more reflection in how you answer the question, *What the heck am I going to do with my life?* than you realize.

THE FAMILY FACTOR

Taking reality television to a new level, MTV's *Date My Mom* features one brave guy who takes three different moms on dates in order to find out more about their daughters. After questioning all three moms at length, the bachelor has to choose the daughter he wants to date without even seeing her picture. At the end of the show, everyone meets up to see which lucky girl he picks.

One of my favorite episodes ends with the two young women who weren't chosen and their moms hugging one another and walking off into the sunset. One of the daughters looks at her mom and asks, "What are we going to do now?" Without hesitating, the mom replies, "Well, we're just going to go find you a nice Jewish boy."

I can't help but laugh. I grew up with a Jewish grandmother who always hoped that I would end up with a nice Jewish boy too.[2]

Whether you are aware of it or not, your family has a tremendous impact on how you answer the question, *What the heck am I going to do with my life?* Through their reactions and responses, both stated and unstated, your family provides a framework for approval and acceptance. They not only give you roots; they give context to your life.

Mothers and fathers naturally dream about what their children will grow up to be and accomplish. Often unknowingly, parents project unrealized dreams onto their offspring. Sean, a thirty-year-old, says that as a child he wanted to be a fighter pilot, just like his dad. He notes the influence of his father on his life: "He was a fighter pilot and probably about my age now, in his early thirties, and his whole life was before him, lots of adventure to live and lots of fun to have. He would tell me, 'Son, you can do anything you set your mind to. It doesn't matter what you do in life as long as you put your heart into it and do it with excellence.'"

But around the age of twelve, Sean decided he wanted to become a lawyer. "At that time, my father would have been in his early forties. Life wasn't everything he expected. Flying fighter jets had become a job, not an adventure. The world wasn't any different to him than it had been when he had set out to change it in his early twenties; maybe it was even a little worse. The bureaucracy of the Canadian military had embittered him, and he had begun drinking just a bit more. Life was difficult to deal with, and not knowing how to change it for his son, he said, 'If you want to make it in this world, you need money. The only way to do that is to become a doctor, dentist, or lawyer.'"

Sean didn't like biology or the idea of putting his hands in someone's mouth for a living, so the decision was obvious. But in college, Sean realized he wasn't lawyer material.

"My dad, now in his late forties, saw that the safest place for his son, the way of the future, was in computers. 'I'm telling you, my son, the future is in computers. Learn that and the world will be yours.'"

Sean began studying computer science and made the dean's list. Just not *that* dean's list. "I had a whopping .5 GPA and was about to be expelled," he recalls. "After a couple of years aimlessly trying to find myself and not knowing what to do, I decided to stop wasting my parents' money and drop out. It was about that time that [I realized] God was pursuing me, and I somehow ended up in the office of a mortgage company applying for a job."

Today, Sean owns a successful mortgage company in

Colorado Springs, Colorado. "I do not blame my father for his advice," he says. "He is truly a good man, and to this day, for many reasons, he remains my hero. The problem with my father at that point in his life was that he didn't know who he was and therefore he couldn't know who I was. He desired safety for me and not to seek out the Lord to see who he had made me to be. I cannot say that I was made to be in mortgage, but I can say that right now at least, I am where I am supposed to be. My ministry is in the marketplace. I am changing lives. Maybe someday I'll get a real job or work somewhere that's important and changing the world . . . but maybe I already am."

Parents play a pivotal role in introducing us to new ideas and concepts. They familiarize us with particular professions or pastimes, and once we are comfortable in an area, we are less likely to venture off into new territory.

> FAST FACT: Statistics show that only 30 percent of family businesses survive to the second generation (Entreprenuer.com).

Some families go one step further than just encouraging their children to pursue a particular career; they actually provide an insta-career by owning a business that their children will inevitably take over one day. If you are in line to inherit the family business, you may have been groomed since your childhood to take over the company that your parents or grandparents built from the ground up. And that makes you one of the lucky—or not-so-lucky—ones. To many, the situation is one to envy—your career path seems clear-cut and your financial security is inevitable—but you may look at the situation differently. You may not feel as though you have much choice in the matter. Along with the business, you inherit challenges, debts, and personnel issues, but no one ever talks about those. You also face high expectations for your future, your position, and your performance. Parental approval can quietly be linked to the success of the business. And that's a lot of pressure for anyone.

Looking back on his childhood, Randy, a forty-two-year-old, says he knew by the time he was in fifth grade that he would be working for his father's company. Randy's father, who had a successful subcontracting business, developed a barbeque sauce business and also managed a four-story historic hotel and a variety of rental properties.

"There was not a time when I did not have a job available to me," Randy recalls. "I was given an amazing amount of responsibility at an early age with the knowledge that my parents trusted my judgment and expected me to lead."

A few days after Randy's high school graduation, his father announced that he had just fired one of the production managers at his barbeque sauce plant. Randy was asked to take over the position until the fall, when he would head off to college.

"One of the greatest compliments I have ever received was my dad telling me in August, as I left for college, 'You really came through for us!'" Randy remembers. "The word I remember was *us*—my parents, my family, the employees, their families, the stockholders."

After graduating from college, Randy returned to the only thing he felt destined to do: managing his father's subcontracting business. Randy was quickly promoted to vice president of the corporation, but shortly after, he felt that he was being called to something more.

"After a great deal of prayer and ten years of hard work, I made the decision to quit running [from] God and go to seminary," he says. "It was one of the most difficult things I have ever had to do."

One of the company's business associates felt so strongly that Randy needed to stay with the company that he offered him the deal of a lifetime: If he would continue to work for the family business for ten years, then the associate would underwrite any business venture Randy chose for up to one million dollars.

Despite the generous offer, Randy enrolled in seminary that fall. Looking back, Randy, now a full-time Presbyterian minister, says, "Although my parents were supportive, I think now that they also had a hard time believing that I could leave behind everything we worked to build. My dream at one point had been to develop a piece of property for residential construction (with the one-million-dollar offer), and someone else did it later on and made a fortune. In my weaker moments I still think about what I turned down, but I am absolutely convinced I made the right choice, more importantly the one God was calling me to do."

Even if you aren't in line to inherit a family business like Randy, you may have been directly or indirectly encouraged to pursue a particular profession through your parents' influence. If your dad always wanted to be an engineer, you may find yourself unknowingly fulfilling his dream by becoming one. Or you may come from a long line of people in a specific profession. The Andersons are always teachers. The Joneses are always plumbers. The Carrys always work in the circus.

I recently met a man who had spent six years in the military because every male in his family had served in the military for the last two hundred years. Even though he wasn't particularly interested in joining the armed services, he readily admitted that he did it so he wouldn't be the "black sheep" of the family.

Sometimes the pressure to join the family profession isn't even mentioned out loud. In fact, you may be encouraged to pursue other areas of study or work. But after graduation or a few years down the road, you find that jobs are easier to come by in your parents' profession because of their connections. You may even be able to land a more lucrative job because of whom they know.

Occasionally peers or friends who become like extended family can also influence a career decision. If you hung with the theater crowd in college, you may be tempted to move to L.A. en masse. Or if you were among the music crowd, you may decide to join the same orchestra.

Of course, not all of the pressures that friends and family exert will be about your profession. You will find all kinds of influences. You may be told whom you should avoid dating, the proper age for marriage, and whether or not it is acceptable to be a stay-at-home mom or dad. Not all this advice is bad, mind you, but it is important to realize that the people around you can play a tremendous role in determining what you do with your life. Sometimes good. Sometimes bad.

> The struggle is to resist the temptation to please others in our career decisions rather than do what we were created to do.

If you wake up one day and realize that friends or family have nudged you in a direction that wasn't your first choice, recognize that God may be trying to speak to you. The changes needed may be slight. They may only affect your heart, not your profession, but they are still important to consider. Spend time in prayer. Take time to listen. Check your motives. Reflect on your past.

YOUR FAMILY'S ROLE

Consciously or subconsciously, your family may have played a bigger role in your career choice than you realize. Take a few minutes to reflect on the following:

Did any of your family members influence your decision to pursue your profession? How so?

_____

_____

_____

_____

_____

_____

Do you feel any expectations from your family
members regarding your current job or future work?
Explain.

_____

_____

_____

_____

_____

_____

What could you accomplish that would make your parent(s)
the proudest?

_____

_____

_____

_____

What—if any—changes do you feel like God is asking you
to make?

_____

_____

_____

_____

_____

THE MONEY FACTOR

ABC's *Life of Luxury* is the eighties classic *Lifestyles of the Rich and Famous* on steroids. Each episode is filled with stars and the rich elite outdoing themselves with excess. A recent episode featured Damon Dash, the hip-hop mogul whose half-a-billion-dollar Roc-A-Fella music and clothing empire helps him maintain his lavish lifestyle, which includes two rather phat pads—a five-thousand-square-foot Tribeca loft in Manhattan and a Beverly Hills mansion. Even with all the glitz and glamour, Dash still knows what's important: He enjoys having a fresh pair of sneakers every day. In fact, he is thought to have the largest sneaker collection in the world.

Dash's footwear fetish seems a little strange until the same episode highlights the owner of Sweet Pea, a one-year-old pooch who receives diamonds, a customized cake, and a lavish party that tops out the dog-day birthday affair at thirty thousand dollars.[3]

Life of Luxury paints a picture of what's possible for a price. But here's another picture: Student loans. Car payments. Mortgage payments. The bills abound. It is not as romantic or splashy as a TV show, but it is the world we live in. It is also the world we are likely to stay in. According to *The Millionaire Next Door,* the odds of having a major windfall such as winning the lottery, landing a multimillion-dollar contract, or becoming the next Mick Jagger (or Bono) are about one in four thousand.[4] Unless you are a member of what my father calls the "lucky sperm club," you are going to have to bring in enough income to support yourself.

No matter how much you try to deny it, money is always a factor when it comes to *What the heck am I going to do with my life?* The extent of influence money should have on our lives is debatable, but the actual influence of money is undeniable. On a pragmatic level, it takes money to keep the electricity turned on and the loan officers away. Money influences all kinds of decisions—career, hobbies, education, and for some, marriage partners. As you consider what you're going to do with your life, recognize that money will play a role in your decisions. For example, if you have a lot of debt, you may need to focus on getting out of debt before pursuing a new profession or making a major life change.

> **Money was meant to lubricate life, not give life meaning.**

You also need to think about your lifestyle in relation to your income. Depending on how much or how little you make, you will establish a lifestyle that you naturally want to maintain. People tend to think about money only in relation to their income. *If I make $_____, then I'll be able to _____.* This kind of thinking only propels a make-more-and-spend-more mentality. Instead, it's important to consider the lifestyle you want to maintain and what it's really going to cost you in terms of energy, relationships, hours at work, and your ability to lead a vibrant and healthy life. While there is nothing wrong with desiring a level of comfort, security, and freedom, we cross the line when it becomes the epicenter of our lives.

WHAT DOES MONEY BUY FOR YOU?

What do you really want from your money? Reflect on the following list and circle the words that describe what money really buys for you.

Security	Importance	Happiness	Reputation
Self-worth	Love	Safety	Control
Self-confidence	Acceptance	Protection	Status
Significance	Acclaim	Well-being	Affirmation
Power	Friends	Position	
Freedom	Approval	Class	

Once you can identify the heartfelt need that you hope money will satisfy, then you can determine how much money drives you. In the space below, draw a picture of what money really buys for you.

Money =

Do you think you have a healthy relationship with money? In what ways are you relying more on money than God to meet your needs? What steps can you take to develop a healthier relationship with money?

On a regular basis, ask yourself, *How much is enough?*

It's a simple question, but it's also a litmus test of what drives us. It's easy to fall into the trap of acquiring things rather than maintaining and improving on the things that truly matter.

Ultimately, the role money plays in your life is largely up to you. A lot depends on what money actually buys for you. In other words, money is rarely an end in and of itself.

THE HERO FACTOR

Heroes have an incredible impact on what we want to do with our lives. From comic books to real-life inspirations, heroes have the ability to lift the lid off what we think is possible. They push us to become something greater than ourselves.

Heroes come in all forms. Some are rich and famous. Others are completely unknown. Neighbors, teachers, bosses, and parents can all become heroes. You may have the opportunity to spend months or years with a hero or just a few moments. Or you may only learn about them through history. But whatever the circumstances, a hero is someone who touches your life in an unmistakable way.

Despite the controversy surrounding his life, Lance Armstrong remains one of my biggest heroes. Though Armstrong doesn't share my faith, I found *It's Not about the Bike: My Journey Back to Life* one of the most spiritually challenging books

I have ever read. The autobiography tells the story of Armstrong's battle with cancer and the extreme sacrifices he made to compete in the Tour de France. He describes the Tour as a metaphor for life—not only as one of the longest races but also as the most exalting, heartbreaking, and potentially tragic race.

Armstrong is one of those rare individuals who sees the glass half full even when it is completely empty. He has an unusual ability to identify the blessing behind adversity. He notes that one of the unexpected benefits of cancer was that the chemotherapy completely reshaped his body. His new lean frame enabled him to climb the mountains with ease and win the Tour de France.

Armstrong says that in addition to redesigning his physical frame, the battle with cancer deeply affected him as an individual. He writes:

The truth is that cancer was the best thing that ever happened to me. I don't know why I got the illness, but it did wonders for me, and I wouldn't want to walk away from it. Why would I want to change, even for a day, the most important and shaping event in my life?[5]

Whoa. Where does he get the wisdom? Where does he get the grace? I pray for such courage and insight and then wonder why I melt down over mild inconveniences. While I am not ready to jump on a bike and race up any hills in France, Armstrong is still a hero because he taught me something about perspective and perseverance that has stayed with me to this day (and it's not about the bike).

My life has been filled with heroes—some who have

become mentors and others who have become friends—and many of them still don't know their impact. A caring and loving fifth grade teacher encouraged me in English. A hardworking speech and debate coach with benchmark integrity poured into my life during high school. A fiftysomething ex-alcoholic-turned-youth pastor became a living, breathing example of Christ for me and hundreds of other teenagers. A magazine editor recognized something in me that I couldn't see in myself and remains a kind, supportive voice in my life. A prominent ministry leader and his wife serve as long-distance mentors to my husband and me.

The Bible talks about heroes too. Elijah was a hero and spiritual leader to Elisha. Samuel provided encouragement and guidance for David. Paul was a hero and mentor to Timothy.

God places people in our lives to be heroes. They become sources of encouragement, hope, and inspiration as we discover who we are and what we're going to do.

PERSONAL HEROES

When you look back over your life for people who really made an impact, who comes to mind? How did they become part of your life? Why did they make such a difference?

Person	How You Met	Impact

Heroes all have one common trait: They awaken something inside of you. Through their lives more than their words, they teach you that you can do something greater than you ever thought possible.

Take a second look at the heroes in your life. What do they have in common?

_____

_____

_____

_____

_____

In what ways do their examples or their words live inside of you today?

_____

_____

_____

_____

_____

What type of person do you want to be a hero to someday (children, teenagers, adults, seniors)? Why?

_____

_____

_____

_____

_____

THE PASSIVITY FACTOR

Las Vegas has developed a rather catchy advertising campaign: "What happens in Vegas, stays in Vegas." For travelers heading to sin city, the promise is inviting—no one back home has to know about the trouble you find or the trouble that finds you. The campaign is brilliant because it applies to everyone. It works for the visitors who are actively seeking an over-the-top good time or those who happen to stumble on one by accident.

Some people by nature are more aggressive than others. Whether they're called type A personalities or go-getters, these individuals have big plans for the future. Watch a single episode of *The Apprentice* and you'll see prime examples of type A's at work. They know where they want to go and what they have to do to get there.

Not everyone has a Red Bull personality. Others are a bit more cool and relaxed—not only in planning a trip to Vegas but also in planning their lives. Not everyone responds aggressively to the question, *What the heck am I going to do with my life?* Some people—by nature or nurture—respond more passively.

The common mantra of the passive person is *whatever happens, happens.* Rather than grab the bull by the horns, they enjoy watching the rodeo of life from the sidelines. Instead of aiming for the top, they find a comfortable place at ground level to wait things out. These individuals may be hardworking and conscientious, but when the door of opportunity opens, they manage to hesitate long enough that it shuts again.

• You've talked about changing jobs for at least a year, but even with invitations from competitive employers to submit a job application, you still haven't taken the time to update your résumé.

• You've wanted to move out of your apartment, condo, or house for months, but despite multiple opportunities to move, you are still living in the same place.

• Rather than develop plans for travel or activities, you rely on a great group of friends or coworkers to organize everything for you.

• Without (fill in the name of a close friend), you practically wouldn't have a social life.

• You've known for some time that you should put together a budget, figure out your finances, and begin saving for the future, but you still haven't gotten around to doing it.

If you answered "that's me" to:

1: You are mostly a go-getter.

2–3: You are extremely laid-back and confident that everything will work out in the end, with or without your input.

4–5: You are excessively relaxed about what goes on in your life to the point that you sometimes allow others to live your life for you.

People who are passive don't live life as much as they allow life to live them. Sometimes situations and events turn out great, and other times they turn into disasters, but for the most part they just turn out. You probably know a few people who respond to life passively. You may even be one.

Passive people are often the kind that you naturally want to be around. Whether you are throwing a tailgate party before the big game or a weekend barbecue, they are standards on the invite list. In fact, passive people are some of my favorite people on the planet. Besides, from time to time even most type A's around us are passive.

But most of the people I know, including myself, are not passive; rather they're passive/aggressive about life. They will allow a certain number of issues or events to roll off their back before they stand up and say *enough,* or they maintain a mental list of issues that they will respond to directly. For example, a person may be passive about their career. They don't care about new opportunities or taking a leadership role; they may not want the responsibility. A solid-paying job with an annual raise is satisfactory. But when it comes to their personal life—whether it is dating, exercise, responding to the needs of others—they're very active and aggressive.

Everyone has areas that naturally concern them. You may have fewer or many more than the people around you, depending on your age and stage in life and personality type. It is important to be aware of your natural response to both obstacles and opportunities.

How do you respond to life? Are you passive, aggressive, or a mixture of both?

_____

_____

In what areas do you need to take more initiative? In what areas do you need to relax so you can conserve your energy and resources for things that are truly important?

_____

_____

_____

THE TALENT FACTOR

As a child, Charles loved to draw and enjoyed the popular characters created by Walt Disney. One of the five-year-old's teachers recognized his talent and proclaimed, "Someday, you are going to be an artist."

Charles eventually studied art, and one of his cartoon panels was published in the _St. Paul Pioneer Press._ A series of rejection letters followed, but Charles kept submitting his work. He finally sold his drawings to the United Feature Syndicate. They renamed the comic strip _Peanuts._

By 1999, _Peanuts_ had grown from its initial debut of seven newspapers in 1950 to more than 2,600 worldwide. Before his death in 2000, Charles Schultz received the Rueben Award, comic art's highest honor, and had been named International Cartoonist of the Year in 1978.

There's little question that Charles Schultz—who introduced Snoopy to the world—was born with natural talent. His talent helped shape the course of his life.

Talent is a significant factor in determining what you choose to do with your life. Everyone—from Charles Shultz to Tiger Woods—likes to do what comes naturally. As children, we are conditioned to expect praise and accolades when we do something particularly well. Strong performances or skills are rewarded with trophies, ribbons, and certificates. As a kid, you may have captivated audiences with your acting, singing, or ability to play basketball. Now that you are an adult, you likely enjoy doing these things because you excel at them and they make you feel good about yourself.

Talents and gifts don't always become just pastimes and hobbies; they can take us one step further in our professions. People with a talent for cooking often become chefs. Those who have a knack with computers find themselves working in Silicon Valley. Those with a gift for dance end up on stage.

Having natural talent that relates to your job is rewarding and betters your chances of success, but it also creates new challenges. Depending on how good you are at what you do, you may find yourself struggling with feelings of pride or superiority. You can also fall into the trap of basing your self-worth on what you do.

WHAT SKILLS DO YOU HAVE AND MOST ENJOY USING?

Generally speaking, all skills can be divided into six clusters or families. To see which ones you are attracted to most, try these exercises. Below is an aerial view of a room where a party is taking place. At this party, people with the same or similar interests have all gathered in the same area of the room as described below:

GROUP A: People who have athletic or mechanical ability, who prefer to work with objects, machines, tools, plants, or animals or to be outdoors.

GROUP B: People who like to work with data, who have clerical or numeric ability, who carry things out in detail or follow through on others' instructions.

GROUP F: People who like to work with people—to inform, enlighten, help, train, develop, or cure them—or are skilled with words.

THE PARTY

GROUP C: People who like to work with people by influencing or persuading, who like to perform, lead, or manage for organizational goals or economic gain.

GROUP D: People who like to observe, learn, investigate, analyze, evaluate, or solve problems.

GROUP E: People who have artistic, innovative, or intuitional abilities and like to work in unstructured situations, using their imagination or creativity.

1. Which area of the room would you instinctively be drawn to? Which group of people would you most enjoy being with for the longest time? (Put aside any question of shyness or whether you would have to talk with them.)
Write the letter for that group here:

2. After fifteen minutes, everyone in the area you have chosen leaves for another party across town. Of the groups that still remain, which would you be drawn to the most? Which group of people would you most enjoy being with for the longest time?
Write the letter for that group here:

3. After fifteen minutes, this group leaves for another party. Of the groups that remain now, which would you be drawn to the most? Which group of people would you most enjoy being with for the longest time?
Write the letter for that group here:

4. Now underline the skills that you like best in each area. The underlined skills in the groups you have selected will indicate the key skill sets you have, enjoy using, and will probably want to "sell" to prospective employers.[6]

God gives every individual a unique blend of talents and gifts that should ideally be used and developed over the course of a lifetime. But sometimes discovering that you don't have a talent for something can help shape your life or at least send it in another direction.

Nicole, a twenty-year-old, got hooked on the idea of working for NASA in third grade after completing a project on Sally Ride, the first American woman in space. "The whole concept of exploring outside of this world was fascinating to me," she says. "I also have vivid memories of visiting the Smithsonian's Air and Space Museum with my parents, so I'm sure this contributed to my fascination with space."

Somewhere around eighth or ninth grade, Nicole realized that science was not one of her strengths, so she began taking language courses, including German. "I had an amazing teacher, who really showed me that learning a language can be fun and fascinating," she recalls. "He showed me that learning a language is not about looking up words in a dictionary, but it is learning a culture and understanding how people are different."

She ended up studying German in college and spent her entire junior year on a scholarship studying at Freie University in Germany. While the experience was rewarding, Nicole says she is now in the process of re-evaluating what she wants to do because the language barrier has been so immense. "I thought the language would come easily to me," she says. "But I really have had a tough time adjusting. I am trying to be patient, knowing that the language will come to me with time, but taking courses and learning the language has been difficult. Maybe once this year is over and my German has improved, I will be able to say that German is my passion, but for now, it is just a point of frustration."

Talent or lack of natural talent has an enormous impact in determining *What the heck am I going to do with my life?* Sometimes talent steers us in a particular direction, and other times it steers us away.

> In the end, talent will only take you so far, and then it is time for hard work, discipline, and perseverance to kick in.

Working in an arena that you are not naturally good at, you are bound to grow stronger, develop character, and learn new skills. At the same time, prepare for frustration and discouragement when things don't go your way.

What are your natural talents and gifts? Make a list of things you do well. What are areas that you've struggled with professionally or academically? Make a second list of things that you don't do well.

Areas of Strength   Areas of Weakness

_____   _____

_____   _____

_____   _____

_____   _____

_____   _____

_____   _____

How has each item you listed in either column helped shape your decisions about what you do so far?

_____

_____

_____

_____

_____

_____

Looking at your work and life right now, in what areas are you maximizing your strengths? In what areas are you operating outside of your natural gifts and talents?

_____

_____

_____

_____

_____

_____

Do you have any talents that you feel you're not utilizing? If so, what steps can you take to begin using them?

_____

_____

_____

_____

_____

_____

THE NEED FACTOR

It doesn't sound like America. Two- and three-room shacks where you can choose any room to be your kitchen, living room, or bathroom because there's nothing there to say otherwise. No running water, no toilets, and no upkeep. Yet the community of Bayview, Virginia, consisted largely of these shacks, which rent for a mere thirty dollars a month.

In 1995, the state of Virginia announced that Bayview would become the home to a new maximum-security prison. Everyone knew it would change the community, but it wasn't the kind of change anyone wanted.

Alice Coles, a forty-five-year-old single mother of two children who was only making five thousand dollars a year handpicking the meat out of crabs, decided to do something about it. She and a group of other residents began lobbying against the prison to county officials. The result of the effort was a new local group known as The Bayview Citizens for Social Justice.

Together, Coles and other Bayview residents who were part of the small organization were able to fight off the prison, but they knew they needed to improve their neighborhood or something worse than a prison was going to come to their town. Eight people from the community became core leaders and learned about starting a nonprofit, budgeting, lobbying, and fund-raising. They developed a new vision and dream for rebuilding the community that included more than 130 new homes, a greenhouse, and a community technology center.

The group lobbied for more than four years before state and federal officials began offering Bayview money. Since 1998, Bayview has raised more than ten million dollars from nearly three dozen state, federal, and private sources. On October 1, 2004, fourteen families were given keys to the homes they had been dreaming about for nearly a decade. Though the homes cost around seventy thousand dollars to build, some will rent for as little as thirty dollars a month because they are subsidized through the U.S. Department of Agriculture's rural poverty program.

Today more than forty-two homes have been built. The Bayview community has seen streetlights go up and driveways paved and watched the building of apartments, offices, and even a Laundromat. Through the compelling vision of Alice Coles, the town of Bayview has been transformed from a Civil War–era African-American community into a modern town with modern housing.[7]

As demonstrated by Alice's story, necessity can play an enormous factor in how you answer the question, *What the heck am I going do to with my life?* You may see a need—one that you may or may not relate to on a personal level—that you can't help but try to meet. You may be especially sensitive to the needs of children, the elderly, the poor, or those with mental or physical challenges.

My husband is particularly aware of the needs of children. He has a huge heart for little ones. He grew up in a family that was overflowing with love and support, but they didn't always have a lot of money. Because he's aware of what it's like to grow up without, he naturally notices children who aren't provided for as much as other kids. On several occasions, he has noticed a child in our church who could really use something— whether it is a new pair of shoes or a bike. He will tenderly ask the parents if he can purchase the item for the child. After receiving the gifts, the kids usually have big smiles on their faces, but the biggest smile belongs to my husband. Responding to kids' specific needs fills him with indescribable joy.

Meeting people's needs is not always about buying them something, though. Sometimes it is a matter of social justice: defending people who cannot defend themselves. When you recognize an injustice, something inside of you compels you to do whatever you can to make it right.

What kinds of needs among other people are you most likely to respond to? What situations or stories make you want to pull out your checkbook or volunteer your time?

_____

_____

_____

What social injustices are you willing to do something about? Record your observations below.

_____

_____

_____

> You were designed to be sensitive to the needs of others, and you
> were called to respond to those needs. Unfortunately, it is not
> always easy to separate the need from the call.

Several years ago, I was working with a small publisher and
debating whether to accept a full-time job offer. The employer
looked at me and said, "The need is the call. We need you here,
so that's obviously where you are supposed to be." I spent
some time wrestling with his words. I finally determined that
while the need can be the call, the need isn't always the call.

We live in a very needy world. If I responded to all the
immediate needs in life, then I wouldn't ever leave my home.
I would be busy responding to basic needs—cleaning, washing, and upkeep of the home. I would answer every e-mail
and return every call immediately. When I found a free
moment, I could branch out to the needs of my neighbors,
but I'd probably never get beyond the house two doors down.

God asks that we discern the need from the call. There are
some needs that are easy to meet. They are no-brainers. If a
person in a wheelchair needs the door held, it is just common
courtesy to help. But before we get involved in big projects,
like full-time ministry, it is important to stop, pray, and make
sure that it is the right place to use our gifts.

Jesus demonstrated this during his three-year ministry. He
encountered multitudes of people with needs, many of which
were physical. Jesus healed some, but the Bible tells us that he
did not heal them all.

In John 5:19, Jesus explains the secret of his discernment process: "I tell you the truth, the Son can do nothing by himself; he can do only what he sees his Father doing, because whatever the Father does the Son also does." Jesus was in such close communion with God the Father that he could discern what needs he was specifically supposed to meet. His words challenge us to be sensitive not only to the needs around us but also to the One who will ultimately meet those needs.

Sometimes responding to necessity isn't about someone else. It is personal. Based on the way you were raised, you may have a need that quietly drives you. You may need to have a sense of personal safety or financial security. You may be looking for the approval that a parent never provided. You may hunger for a sense of status you never felt as a child. Needs that were overlooked or unmet during childhood are likely to reappear in adulthood, and it is important to be aware of the ways they could be influencing your life decisions.

Obviously, everyone needs food, water, and shelter, but push yourself to go one step further in understanding your needs. Make a list of your top five emotional and mental needs.

Emotional Needs:

1. _____
2. _____
3. _____
4. _____
5. _____

Mental Needs:

1. _____
2. _____
3. _____
4. _____
5. _____

Take a moment to reflect. How have these needs been affecting your life decisions?

_____

_____

_____

_____

_____

_____

_____

_____

Which professions and hobbies have these needs steered you toward? Which professions and hobbies have they steered you away from?

Toward: Away From:

_____   _____

_____   _____

_____   _____

_____   _____

_____   _____

_____   _____

_____   _____

_____   _____

THE GOD FACTOR

A few years ago a neighbor visited one of my friends' apartment, where we were all hanging out. He was stressed. He had misplaced his key ring, and now he was locked out of everything—his car, his apartment, his work, his mailbox. It seemed like his entire life was on that little ring. Sitting with his hand on his forehead staring at the floor, he reviewed all the places he had revisited searching for his keys. We all listened patiently and offered to help.

I knew that he and everyone in the room were Christians. I couldn't help but ask, "Have you taken some time to pray and ask God where the keys might be?"

Before I could catch my breath, he snapped back, "God doesn't care about little things like lost keys. Why should I bother asking him where they are?"

"Because he knows where they are!" I replied in one of those I'm-really-not-trying-to-be-religious-though-that's-what-it-sounds-like-right-now moments.

Looking back, it probably wasn't the best timing. In fact, it took him another two days to find his keys. But I couldn't help it. I was all too familiar with his situation. Even with a nice little chrome key-ring holder next to my front door, I have a chronic problem with misplacing my keys. Just ask my husband. They are constantly disappearing. I have copies of my car key all over the house and a few stashed with friends and relatives just in case. I'm an expert on lost keys. The only thing that has worked for finding my keys is prayer. I will search for hours for a single set; then when I remember to stop and pray, they mysteriously reappear. It is a lesson I have learned again and again.

It's too bad I haven't figured out how to apply that lesson to other areas of my life. If God knows everything—including my car key's latest location—then certainly he knows a thing or two about the future.

The God factor should be the biggest factor in determining *What the heck am I going to do with my life?* because God is ultimately the One who knows you best. The Bible says he fashioned you in your mother's womb (Isaiah 44:2; Psalm 139:13-16) and designed every detail of your DNA. He knows your strengths and weaknesses, your likes and dislikes. God knows the environments in which you will develop, grow, and become more like him.

Part of God's nature is that he is a shepherd. He is a guide. James 1:5 is shooting straight when it says if we're at a loss for what to do, we're to go to God who gives wisdom generously. James goes so far as to say that God will not only provide the wisdom but do it without finding fault. In other words, God's grace and love cover us when we've lost our way.

By nature, God wants to offer guidance, but recognizing the different ways he speaks and leads isn't always easy. It begins with asking God for direction. That may seem like a pretty small step, but it requires big faith and quite a bit of humility.

When was the last time you got lost when you were driving somewhere? For me, it's almost a way of life. Whether I use MapQuest, OnStar, or get an intensely detailed set of directions over the phone, I still manage to get lost. Knocking on a stranger's door to ask for directions doesn't just take humility, it also takes courage. In the same way, we sometimes find ourselves a little lost on this journey we call life. Thank goodness God isn't a stranger. Asking God for help implies that we don't have all the answers. It acknowledges that we are not in control of our own lives and we are dependent on someone else for guidance. Asking God for direction is an expression of humility, and according to that verse in James, he can't help but respond.

> When you are asking God for direction, you have to remember to stay put long enough to listen for an answer.

This can be one of the most challenging parts of figuring out what to do next. After praying about a situation, I'll usually spend some time reading the Bible, a book that serves as God's megaphone to his people. It's a book that's packed with wisdom, insight, direction, and some funky maps of the Middle East in the back.

While you won't find a specific verse that tells you whether you're called to be a nuclear scientist, day-care worker, or Avon representative, you are likely to find comfort, encouragement, and insight about what God is doing in this season of your life. You may also discover that what you really thought you wanted to do—whether working as Ashton Kutcher's personal assistant or maintaining quality control at Godiva—isn't exactly what God has in mind. He may (believe it or not) have something even better.

Getting into the Bible can be tough stuff. A ton of easily torn, thinly printed pages may leave you wondering where to begin. I'm partial to studying the Gospels and the life of Christ. Sometimes I'll read the books of Matthew, Mark, Luke, and John and just read the red letters—the words of Jesus—to connect with him. Other times I'll read the Psalms or meditate on the Proverbs. And occasionally, I'll play Bible roulette and read the pages that naturally fall open. Sometimes God uses the strangest little verses to speak directly into my life.

Remember that God is creative and colorful, and he can use not only the Bible, but some other means to get your attention. He may speak to you through wise Christian friends, pastors, or even your parents. He could respond to your need for direction through circumstances—opening or closing the doors to certain opportunities. He can speak to you through a song, book, movie, or even your personal time of journaling. Or God may nudge you through the Holy Spirit who lives inside of you. You could find yourself thinking a thought you know can't be your own or have a desire that you just can't shake.

You may also find that God begins addressing issues in your life that are completely unrelated to your current job or vocation.

> As you seek God's will for your life—whether it is concerning a job or not—recognize that he is calling you to faithfulness in everything you do, not just the nine-to-five grind.

As you ask God for direction, here are a few questions to consider:

Does what I heard line up with Scripture?

Does what I heard line up with circumstance?

Does what I heard line up with wise counsel?

Does what I heard leave me with a sense of peace?

It may take weeks, months, or even years for God's leading to become clear. As you seek God, pray, and listen for his voice, he will lead you. Once you sense that nudge to move forward, be obedient. If you hear from God but don't obey, then you've only gone halfway. Your follow-through is essential.

If you don't feel like you've heard anything, remain patient. Don't rush. Don't feel like you have to jump into something. If you are cornered into making a decision, pray, ask for wise counsel, and choose the option that seems best. Many people become paralyzed by fear of making the wrong decision. They're so consumed with seeking God's will that they avoid actively pursuing his will.

One of the best analogies I have heard came from a friend who said that finding God's will is a lot like being trapped in a giant hotel. Some people spend their entire lives going from floor to floor trying to find the right room. They never stop to realize that just by being in the building, they're already in the right place.

When you are in a close relationship with God, you are in the right place—no matter where you are physically located. The Kingdom of God isn't hinging on whether you take a part-time job at the donut shop or the barbershop. God can use you in both places. And if your place of employment really is that crucial, then don't you think God will be able to ensure you get the job at the right store?[8]

Sometimes God's direction is full of surprises. Cathy, a thirty-nine-year-old, graduated with an elementary education degree and special education certification. "I was going to teach in an elementary classroom but ended up teaching special education," she says. "There were several years when I taught special education in the mornings at a public school and then taught math and language arts in a Christian school in the afternoons. After we moved, I thought I'd teach, but I ended up working at an espresso shop. Now I'm an office manager at a college. I never thought I'd be doing what I'm doing right now. The place I feel the least comfortable is as a secretary. I may think I know what I want to do with my life, but God doesn't always see it like that."

God may just surprise you with his plan for your life, too.

FACTORING IN THE FACTORS

God should be the primary factor when it comes to figuring out *What the heck am I going to do with my life?* and he is also the One who ties all the other factors together to direct you. Sometimes God uses your family or a personal role model to steer you toward a particular profession. Sometimes he uses a need or an issue of social justice to point you in a certain direction. Even the desire to make money can be used by God, particularly when the money will be used to benefit others. And sometimes God will give you a passion or a natural talent for something that he's uniquely created you to do.

Take some time to reflect on the different factors that have influenced your life to date.

Place circles around each factor listed below that has influenced your life. Place stars beside the factors that have had the most influence.

- Family Factor
- Money Factor
- Need Factor
- Hero Factor
- Talent Factor
- Passivity Factor
- God Factor
- Other Factors?

Do you see a pattern in the way God has been directing you?

_____

_____

_____

_____

_____

_____

_____

In what ways has God used your family, heroes, financial
needs, and talents to push you?

_____

_____

_____

_____

_____

_____

_____

That's-Oh-So-Random Job Stats:

It's estimated that ten years after receiving a diploma, 80 percent of college graduates are working in a field unrelated to their majors.

A study by the Families and Work Institute found that younger workers are more "family-centric" or "dual-centric" (with equal priorities on both career and family) and less "work-centric" (putting higher priority on their jobs than families) than members of the baby boom generation.

A recent survey by *Gallup Management Journal* found that 19 percent of the nation's workers not only are not enthralled or excited by their work, but they are "actively disengaged," meaning they're fundamentally disconnected from it.

According to the University of Warwick, overall job-satisfaction scores have dropped in the United States in each of the previous three decades. In the 1970s, 56 percent of Americans were extremely satisfied at work. In the 1980s, it was 52 percent. In the 1990s, 47 percent were satisfied.

The Centers for Disease Control and Prevention estimates that 90 percent of doctor visits in the United States may be triggered by stress-related illness.

Calling:

What Pulls You?

The place God calls you to is the place where your deep gladness and the world's deep hunger meet.

Frederick Buechner

Ken Frantz sat in the waiting room of a Ford car dealership in Virginia while his truck was being serviced. Slightly bored, Ken picked up a four-month-old *National Geographic* magazine, which just happened to be the closest publication in reach. He flipped to an article about the first rafting expedition down the entire Nile River. The image on the page instantly captivated him. The spectacular photograph featured a very old bridge in Ethiopia that had been severely damaged and never repaired. Villagers on either side used a sagging rope to carry human cargo back and forth. Ken looked at the man hanging by a loop on the tired and frayed rope. If the man or the rope slipped, he would fall to his death on the rocks below.

"I was born to see this photo, understand it, and know what I needed to do," Ken recalls. "I was supposed to build that bridge."

Ken returned home and began making phone calls. He tracked down the photographer who took the picture for *National Geographic* and shared his idea. She thought it was incredible. Ken decided to phone the deputy ambassador of Ethiopia.

"Imagine getting some call from some crazy nut who says he's going to go fix a bridge," Ken says. "I'd [just] refer the call somewhere and pass it off. But instead, [the ambassador] was totally into solving the problem. He figured out how to get me into the country as a tourist, because we weren't an NGO [nongovernmental organization]."

Ken made another call to his brother, Forrest, who lived in the Seattle area. He started sharing his idea for rebuilding the bridge.

In the middle of the conversation, Forrest stopped him and asked, "Are you talking about the picture in the *National Geographic* magazine?"

"That's it," Ken replied.

"I remember seeing that article," Forrest explained. "And I had the exact same thought."

In May 2000, Ken, Forrest, and Forrest's son flew to a remote location in Ethiopia to survey the gorge. More than a dozen villages lined each side of the river, bringing the total population of the immediate vicinity to over five hundred thousand. Using translators, Ken spoke with the different tribal elders. "They shared their connection to the bridge and how important it is," he says. "They explained how people can't go to weddings on the other side and how people used to own land on the other side but couldn't farm it without a bridge. They estimated that ten to twenty people were dying each year when the rope pulley broke free.

"This particular area is Orthodox Christian, which is closely related to the Coptic Church in Egypt. The elders were supportive. In every elder group, there's always some-one who is head and shoulders above the rest in terms of their ability to communicate. Two such people made the statement, 'When I see it with my eyes, I can die in peace.'"

Ken returned home and began sharing his idea to build a bridge with others. In February 2001, he returned to Ethiopia. He financed 75 percent of the project himself with an additional 25 percent from friends and family.

Halfway through the bridge-building project, while sitting in his tent one night, Ken says he "discovered faith and came to know God and Jesus in one fell swoop."

Ken's vision eventually led to the creation of Bridges to Prosperity, and today its goals have expanded from simply building bridges to empowering the local people to construct their own. The organization establishes local capacity for footbridge design and construction in the poorest countries of the world through on-the-job training of local villagers and fabricators. "To build bridges, we must first build communities by teaching them on-the-job how to pool their resources and labor to build a bridge on their own," Ken explains. "Basically, we go into a village and help them form a mini public works department."

After each group is formed and trained and actually builds the bridge, it can continue with other public works projects such as water, sanitation, schools, and roads. Building bridges, in other words, is the catalyst for governance, empowerment, self-dependence, and improvements in the standard of living.

Bridges to Prosperity currently operates a bridge program

in Ethiopia with another to begin soon in South America, where many 30- to 100-meter cable-suspension footbridges are in various stages of completion.

"I have talked to many people that are envious," Ken says. "[They say], 'How incredibly lucky you are that you have had this calling.' Sheri, my wife, sees the calling as the way I found Christ. Looking back, I realized that everything prepared me perfectly to do this. I'm not a bridge engineer. A bridge engineer would not have been the best person to have this calling. The project needed someone to operate as an executive director; it had to be someone with logistics experience."[1]

Through an old *National Geographic* magazine, Ken Frantz received a life-changing calling, and his story serves as a reminder that God can use anything and anyone at any time to accomplish his purposes.

RECOGNIZING THE CALL

In many Christian circles, the word *calling* is thrown around like confetti. As I was growing up, the word *calling* was most often used for men and women who were called into full-time church ministry. But lately *calling* is used in all kinds of scenarios. Everything can become a calling of sorts. People are called to certain places, jobs, and even seasons in life. It is no wonder there's so much confusion about the word.

Theologically speaking, *calling* is used to express the idea that God "calls" us to salvation, wooing us to the Good News of Jesus. In other words, calling is about responding to the invitation to be in a relationship with God via his Son, Jesus—

not in an I-signed-a-three-by-five-card-so-I'm-in-the-club kind of way, but in a real, authentic, mud-meets-master-potter kind of encounter.

In that type of relationship with God, calling isn't so much about us as it is about him. Rather than focusing on our own earthly weaknesses and failures, we are caught up in the hope of the One who is creating something new.

When asked what the greatest commandment is, Jesus replied, "'Love the Lord your God with all your heart and with all your soul and with all your mind.' This is the first and greatest commandment. And the second is like it: 'Love your neighbor as yourself'" (Matthew 22:37-39).

```
                              P
                              R
                              I
                              M
                              A
          SECONDARY  CALLING
                              Y

                              C
                              A
                              L
                              L
                              I
                              N
                              G
```

This one Scripture outlines the Christian life. Our primary calling is to love God with everything within us. Then our secondary calling is to manifest our love of God not only in what we do but also to those we come in contact with.

I love what John Piper says in his book *Don't Waste Your Life:*

God's purpose for my life was that I have a passion for God's glory and that I have a passion for my joy in that glory, and that these two are one passion. . . . God created me—and you—to live with a single, all-embracing, all-transforming passion—namely, a passion to glorify God by enjoying and displaying his supreme excellence in all the spheres of life. Enjoying and displaying are both crucial. If we try to display the excellence of God without joy in it, we will display a shell of hypocrisy and create scorn or legalism. But if we claim to enjoy his excellence and do not display it for others to see and admire, we deceive ourselves, because the mark of God-enthralled joy is to overflow and expand by extending itself into the hearts of others. The wasted life is the life without a passion for the supremacy of God in all things for the joy of all peoples.[2]

In other words, we are called to glorify God in all that we do, whether that is flipping burgers, feeding the homeless, or running a Fortune 500 company. When your understanding of calling expands beyond a single job or career path, you are able to live a more integrated life that reflects both your unique personality and your faith. Your faith is more freely reflected in what you do, and what you do will reflect your faith no matter what job title you list on a résumé.

According to Os Hillman, founder and president of International Coalition of Workplace Ministries and Marketplace Leaders, one of the most common misunderstandings people have about calling is the idea that one calling has more value than another. "I think society has placed a hierarchy on the spiritual value of a calling," Hillman says. "This is not biblical. The pastor, missionary, or vocational worker is perceived as the most holy calling, [and] this impacts Christians greatly on how others perceive their life in spiritual terms."

The result is that people fail to see their work outside a church building as a place of outreach and transformation. A job becomes just another job, rather than a place to reflect Christ and his Kingdom.

> When we fall into the mind-set that a ministry role—whether it is as a preacher or a church worker—has more value than a secular role, we discount the real value of what God can do through his people.

Hillman says the second most common misunderstanding is that calling is a onetime event. "We can know our purpose in life to some degree early," he says, "but ultimately, it is learned by looking back over our life."[3]

Mariam, a twenty-six-year-old, describes the impact her father, an orthopedic surgeon, had on her understanding of calling, faith, and the workplace. She grew up noticing the copies of *Our Daily Bread,* a popular devotional, in his waiting room for people to take freely. In addition to offering to pray with patients, Mariam's father would take time to listen to each patient's worries and fears, explain the medical procedures in detail, and treat every patient as a person with dignity.

"I still meet people now whom he operated on in 1980 or so who remember him with deep love and respect because he was such a model of Christ and treated them with such dignity," Mariam says. "He has brought more people than I can count to the Lord merely because he was willing to let Christ's love flow through him in his daily work. I see him as more living out a holy vocation merely because he let his vocation be God's workplace."

Whether they are Ken Frantz building bridges on the other side of the planet or Mariam's dad, there are some people whose lives seem infused with a sense of calling in relation to what they do.

In what ways do you see your job as a place of outreach and transformation? How do you think God wants to use you right where you are?

_____

_____

_____

_____

_____

_____

CALLED OR DRIVEN?

In *Ordering Your Private World,* Gordon MacDonald explores the difference between people who are driven and those who are called. He notes that far too many of us have a quality of "drivenness"—a motivation that causes us to do things for less-than-the-best reasons. Whether we're driven to prove ourselves, earn acceptance, or obtain power for the sake of being powerful, there's an unmistakable edge to what we are doing. Driven people stand in contrast to those who are called and seem to have died to themselves enough to respond to their Creator and what he created them to do with an attitude of humility and grace.

Have you ever taken time to reflect on what drives you?

In what areas of your life do you sense that you're driven (doing something—even a good thing—for the wrong reasons)?

_____

_____

_____

_____

_____

_____

In what areas of your life do you sense that you're called (doing something for the right reasons)?

_____

_____

_____

_____

_____

_____

What changes do you need to make in your attitudes, work habits, and spiritual life to live like a called person rather than a driven person?

_____

_____

_____

_____

_____

_____

DESTINED FOR WHAT?

The process of discovering your calling raises the question of destiny. Is destiny something God orchestrates for us? And if so, what role do we play in discovering that destiny? What is our responsibility?

These are questions I'm still struggling with. If I think about the idea of destiny too long, I'm tempted to take the whole issue out of God's hands and into my own. Somehow the search to find "my destiny" becomes like a quest for the Holy Grail. And that's a lot of pressure for anyone—even Monty Python.

That's when I turn to the biblical story of Ruth and her encounter with Boaz. The story begins as Ruth, a recent widow, chooses to follow her widowed mother-in-law, Naomi, to Bethlehem. Once they arrive, Ruth goes to look for food. The story follows:

And Ruth the Moabitess said to Naomi, "Let me go to the fields and pick up the leftover grain behind anyone in whose eyes I find favor."

Naomi said to her, "Go ahead, my daughter." So she went out and began to glean in the fields behind the harvesters. *As it turned out,* she found herself working in a field belonging to Boaz, who was from the clan of Elimelech. (Ruth 2:2-3, emphasis added)

Boaz is a distant relative of Naomi, and after several encounters, Boaz marries Ruth and they both end up being ancestors to Jesus. It is a beautiful story of God's redemptive purposes. It also reveals how God can use our everyday activities and work to accomplish his will. The Hebrew word for "as it turned out" as used in this context is *miqreh,* and it means "destiny." It implies that God was at work behind the scenes.

Reflecting on the story, I can't help but wonder what would have happened if Ruth had chosen to search for grain in a different field. Scripture doesn't tell us. But God's presence is evident in the turn of events. In fact, in this short book of the Bible you'll discover that the main character isn't Ruth, Boaz, or Naomi. It's God. It is about him and his longing and desire to redeem mankind.

If you look at the overall idea of destiny in Scripture and avoid all the pitfalls and pitchforks that come with the debate over predestination, the idea of destiny isn't as much about this world as it is about the world to come.

> While people are given passions and callings, destiny is about something much more than just a career or vocation, something far more eternal: a relationship with God.

Jesus said, "In my Father's house are many rooms; if it were not so, I would have told you. I am going there to prepare a place for you" (John 14:2). Jesus knew that neither his nor our ultimate destiny is found in this world; it is in the world to come.

Destiny is a journey—one that we're already on whether we realize it or not. The good news is that destiny is something that happens to you; you don't happen to destiny. In other words, the very nature of destiny requires that someone or something greater than you is at work. Your destiny is out of your control. And that's a good thing.

This is a lesson well taught in C. S. Lewis's book *The Horse and His Boy* from the Chronicles of Narnia. The book tells the story of Shasta, who grew up believing he was the son of a poor fisherman in Calormene country, far to the south of Narnia and Archenland. One night, after overhearing that he is not the fisherman's son, Shasta runs away in the company of a talking horse who had been stolen from Narnia.

After many adventures, Shasta finally reaches Archenland just in time to warn the people of an imminent invasion. In doing so, he fulfills the destiny foretold at his birth: He would one day save Archenland from the worst danger it had ever faced.

It was a destiny of which Shasta, really the son of the king of Archenland, was unaware, having been kidnapped shortly after the prophecy was made. And it was a destiny he fulfilled in a frail, fallible, completely human way. In the beginning he was aware only that he did not belong where he was, and later, he was aware only that someone had to warn the king. So by doing what only he could do at each stage, Shasta fulfills his destiny and finds it to be much larger than he had ever dreamed.

I believe with all my heart that God has called and destined this generation to great things. Those "great" things may not be what the world magnifies, but they are the very activities that the One who knows true greatness holds in high esteem.

The question that you have to answer today and every day is how you will respond to his invitation. Those who have the courage to answer the call to live a life glorifying to God no matter what the vocation will have to deafen their ears to the naysayers and ignore those who say it can't be done, it doesn't matter, and you could be doing so much more with your life. Those who answer the call will have to cling to the knowledge and hope that obedience to Christ is everything and learn to work, play, serve, and respond for an audience of One. Indeed, many who live a life of great service will receive the fewest accolades and the least attention from peers. But by answering the call, you will learn to live by faith, walk boldly, run courageously, and rest in the arms of the Savior.

I'm struggling to do this each day in my own life and pray that you will join me on the journey.

What Type Are You?

Did you know that an upholstery repairman actually contributed to the discovery of type A and type B personalities? Cardiologists Meyer Friedman and Ray Rosenman realized that their heart patients were not only emotionally but also physically anxious after an upholstery worker observed that the seats of many of the chairs in their waiting room were worn only on the front. Friedman and Rosenman used the observation as a starting point to study behavior patterns. They discovered two basic types of behavior. Check the words that best describe you.

○ Competitive	○ Relaxed
○ Hardworking	○ Less devoted to work
○ Go-getter	○ Balanced
○ Work oriented	○ Steady
○ Impatient at times	○ Patient
○ Driven	○ Accepting
○ Motivated	○ Agreeable
○ Efficient	○ Indifferent at times
○ Strong sense of time urgency	○ Lenient

If the majority of your selections are in the left column, you're most likely a type A personality. You're devoted to work, often putting in extra hours and going above and beyond. You naturally tend to excel in your workplace and take on increased responsibility. You're a go-getter, and you're often self-driven and self-motivated. You're most likely to become a star employee or manager, though at times you can't help but think about becoming president or CEO.

If the majority of your selections are in the right column, you're most likely a type B personality. You do your job, but you know when to call it quits and go home at the end of the day. You get along with most of your fellow employees and you naturally take a more relaxed and balanced approach to life. People describe you as steady and enjoy your laid-back perspective.

While most people tend to lend themselves to one personality type or the other, different situations, responsibilities, or environments will allow a person to shift toward the other personality type. Interestingly, both personality types are just as likely to succeed in the workplace. While type A's may be driven to succeed, their single focus can alienate them from coworkers as well as lead to burnout later in life. Meanwhile, type B's may find themselves excelling—particularly in management—because of their stronger interpersonal skills and relationships.*

*Adapted from Organizational Behavior: Managing People and Organizations by Gregory Moorhead and Ricky W. Griffin (New York: Houghton Mifflin, 2004), 222-24.

Passion:

What Makes You Fly Inside?

I hunger for the comfort that can come from devotion to herd wisdom. Yet, at the same time, I remain desperate to flee the soul-wilting thatch of society's rules and standards and fly to the more uncertain but broader possibilities of living originally.

Gordon MacKenzie

Passion is something that runs through your veins. It goes beyond just getting your attention; it is able to keep it. When you pursue something that you are passionate about, you tap into a reservoir of strength and hope. You keep going when others quit. You remain optimistic when others see nothing but signs of failure. You are compelled by something greater than yourself.

Bill Stoffregen's passion led him into horticulture. Raised on a farm in Raleigh, North Carolina, Bill was always fascinated by plants. After graduating from high school, he attended North Carolina State University and studied forestry. He worked for the next eleven years for the North Carolina Division of Forestry. Meanwhile, he pursued his passion for growing plants. The hobby eventually became a business, and Bill and his wife opened Homewood Nursery and Garden Center. The business consists of two acres of covered greenhouses, a garden center, a nursery sales yard, and a gift area. Today the family business is run by their two sons and employs around fifty people.

Bill and his wife also pursued another passion: their relationship with Christ. Following a strong pull to serve God, they used the slow season at the nursery to serve in short-term missions around the world through Youth With A Mission. Over the last thirty-five years, they have traveled to South Korea, the Philippines, the Dominican Republic, and Guatemala.

In 2000, Bill took a trip to Mauretania, Africa, where he observed the extreme poverty and need. "Although I had been to so many third-world countries, I don't think anything could have prepared me for what lay before me in Mauretania," Bill says. "There was poverty and filth everywhere. There were people with no hope. In the refugee camp that we worked in, the average income for a family was fifty cents a day."

Because of Bill's natural interest in plants, he couldn't help but notice that the land was a "horticultural nightmare." The extreme wind and lack of rain made the land inhospitable for growth. "There were no plants, only dry, windblown sand," Bill recalls. "Except there was this one little species of tree that seemed to be thriving." The green foliage of these trees was easy to spot in a sea of nothing. Naturally curious, Bill asked the interpreter about the species of the trees.

"Oh, that's a neem tree," the interpreter replied nonchalantly.

Bill was intrigued. When he returned home, he began researching neem trees. "I got on the Internet and found more out about neem trees than you would ever want to know," he says.

Six months later, he returned to Mauretania armed with information. He ended up at the University of Nouakchott with the head of botany and biology, who suggested a study on the prevalence and potential of the neem tree in Mauretania. The Stoffregens funded the fifteen-thousand-dollar study out of their own pocket.

On a third trip to Mauretania in July 2001, Bill learned that the tree offered enormous potential to the native people. The fruit of neem trees contains a low-toxicity ingredient that can be harvested and exported. The insecticide made from the fruit kills malaria-causing mosquitoes and controls the locust problem that destroys the few crops the Mauretanian people produce. The massive root systems of the trees help stop the desert's growth in the region. In addition, planting and harvesting neem trees produces jobs and income for the local people. For the people of Mauretania, it is truly a tree of life.

Bill and several others are currently in the early stages of planning a processing plant for the neem trees. He hopes to raise the funds to start a nursery with the University of Nouakchott and produce neem seedlings.

At sixty-eight, Bill says that life continues to be full of excitement. "I will serve the Lord in Mauretania or wherever he sends me as long as he can use me. One thing I have learned is nothing in your life that you have done or learned is ever wasted. God can always use it. Whoever thought that my knowledge in horticulture could be used in faraway Africa? If you ever ask God, 'Why am I here?' then he will tell you."[1]

While horticulture and neem trees may not be your areas of interest, you may still be able to identify with Bill's passion. When you are passionate about something, you tend to notice it wherever you go. It makes you feel more alive. It is easy to recognize a person's passion. When they begin talking about it, their eyes light up. Not only do they know a lot about the topic, but they're thrilled to have someone express an interest in knowing more about it. They usually begin talking more quickly. Some people actually trip over their own words as they discuss their passion. It is something they cannot contain.

WHAT IS YOUR PASSION?

For some, the answer comes easily. You know your passion and you've always known. It might be a hobby or pastime or profession, but ever since you were a little child, you have had an interest in _____. Or you've always wanted to be a _____. Even now, many years later, you are still taking the classes or making the time or working to fulfill that desire.

For others, their passion isn't quite as clear. It is more of a notion, an inkling or a leaning toward something. It is a compelling.

When I asked my friend Corrine about her passion, she stared at me blankly. "I just don't think I'm a very passionate person," she replied. "I'm fairly laid-back. I just don't get excited about many things."

"How do you feel when you're out in the woods?" I asked, referring to her job studying salmon with the USDA Forest Service.

"There are some days when I'm out in the field and I think, 'Wow, I'm getting paid for this!'"

"I think you know your passion, and you're doing it," I replied.

"I think you're right," she answered.

> Passion is not to be confused with exuberance. Just because you're not a naturally excitable or energetic person does not mean you don't have a passion.

In the first chapter, I mentioned a question that helped me realize my passion for writing: If I could do anything with my life, assuming that time and money were no object, what would I choose to do?

Take a moment and reflect on your own life.

If you could do anything with your life, assuming that time and money were no object, what would you choose to do?

_____

_____

_____

_____

Maybe you knew the answer instantly. Or maybe you are among the many people I've talked to who said they had read the question and thought about it for some time but still didn't have an answer. What then?

Discovering your passion isn't always easy. Sometimes it is hard to recognize what you really want to do. If you are struggling, here are some questions to consider:

What are your natural talents and gifts?

_____

_____

_____

What do you love to talk and read about the most?

_____

_____

_____

What are the things you do that receive the most compliments?

_____

_____

_____

What interests you professionally?

_____

_____

_____

What professions have you tried that just didn't work for you?

_____

_____

_____

What didn't work for you about those job situations?

_____

_____

_____

If you could do anything to help others, what would you do?

_____

_____

_____

What Are Your Natural Talents and Gifts?

God created each of us with a unique personality that tends toward the more creative, more analytical, more musical, more practical, etc., and when we pursue things that are naturally interesting to us, God can use that interest to lead us in the direction he wants us to go. But recognizing your talents and gifts can be harder than you think. A year after I graduated from college, I decided that I wanted to pursue writing, but it wasn't until several years later that I looked back and realized that writing was something I had been enjoying since my childhood.

In fourth grade, I remember my favorite teacher, Mrs. Stahl, announcing that we would have a countywide book fair and that each of us would write a book. My eyes lit up! I went home and began writing. I wrote a fictional account of a family living on a boat and their encounters with modern-day pirates. By the time I finished the adventure and my gracious mom typed it, my story was 128 pages long. When

I attended the book fair, the other children and their parents looked at me in disbelief. Most of the kids had taken a few sheets of paper, folded them in half, stapled them, and written a few lines with pictures. I probably would have done the same, except no one told me it could be that simple. I just assumed the project had to look like a book, and all the books I had ever seen were thick.

Motivated by a need for scholarship money, I entered all types of essay contests in high school. Looking back years later, I realized that writing didn't just suddenly come into my life; it had been there all along.

Is there anything that you've been doing all along that you didn't realize? This may be a signpost of where God is leading you in the future.

You may have an inclination toward art, science, or literature. You may be interested in how things are put together or taken apart. You may enjoy making people, places, and things more beautiful. Or you may like being creative or methodical in what you do. Maybe you just love kids or you have a knack for computers or you've always wanted to learn how to make pottery. Maybe you love to play an instrument or write songs. Maybe you love learning, and when everyone is in bed at night, you are up until 3 A.M. watching the History Channel. Maybe you love cooking, and for you it is more than just making a meal—it is an art form. Whatever the compelling, you can't escape it. You have hints of talents, gifts, and interests to which you can't help but respond.

When you look back over your life, do you see a common thread of interest or talent?

_____

_____

_____

_____

_____

Stephanie, a thirty-two-year-old, says that she found insight through the book *Let Your Life Speak* by Parker J. Palmer. "[The book] talked about how you can find themes in your childhood play or interests to what you are cut out or called to do because childhood's when you do what you'd do without all the inhibitions and 'shoulds' that you learn as you grow up," she says. "This made me think about how I used to make these elaborate towns out of blocks and 'little people' or out of LEGOs. I wasn't so much interested in, say, the hospital by itself but the hospital and the gas station and the airport and the grocery store and the little houses—all of them together."

Stephanie says that this concept continues in her current job as the head of residence life at a local college. "I'd say this translates into what I do because I really like to help create community in residence life—where people and groups interact with each other in healthy ways and learn good life lessons about how to act and treat others that will do them a world of good in life. I want to help people 'fit together' with others or with God or with their surroundings."

What Do You Love to Talk and Read about Most?

Interests reveal a lot about a person. What magazines do you subscribe to? On an Internet news site, which types of headlines are most likely to make you click? Which channels do you watch on television? What topics in your conversations with friends get you worked up? Pay attention to what subjects naturally pique your interest. They are small windows into your gifts, talents, and passions.

What Are the Things You Do That Receive the Most Compliments?

Your friends, family, and coworkers can often unknowingly help you recognize your talents and skills. They see things in you that you can't see in yourself. When you hear affirming words from several sources (besides your mom) about something you've done, it may be a sign that you have a knack for it.

What Interests You Professionally?

You may be drawn to a particular profession or find yourself in a career that sparks your interest in something else. For example, if you are working as a dental hygienist, you could decide that you'd rather be selling medical products, or vice versa. People begin in one career and shift gears all the time. Police officers become firemen. Lawyers go back to school for their MBA. Hobbies become full-time businesses. Take some time to reflect on your professional interests and remember that it is never too late to try something new.

What Professions Have You Tried That Just Didn't Work for You?

Sometimes you'll try a job and it just doesn't work out. I once worked for a doctor's office in data entry. It didn't last more than a few weeks. I was bored out of my mind, and I wanted to do something—anything—else. I was miserable. And I quickly crossed *data entry* off my list as a possible future job no matter how much it paid. Whether you've tried one or a dozen jobs that didn't work for you, don't be discouraged. Discovering what your passion *isn't* can bring you one step closer to discovering what it is.

What Didn't Work for You about Those Job Situations?

Consider the jobs that you haven't enjoyed. What are the common traits? What was it about the environment, coworkers, management, or tasks that you didn't enjoy? What, if anything, did you enjoy about the job?

If You Could Do Anything to Help Others, What Would You Do?

When you think of giving your time, energy, and talents to others, what naturally comes to mind? If you could volunteer in any organization, which one would you choose? If you were to volunteer in a church, what would you want to do? You may have a common answer—whether it is using your vocal talents or volunteering in the nursery—or you may desire to do something a little offbeat. Since the only solos I'm willing to sing are so low that you'll never hear me because I can't hold a tune, I bake cookies and cakes for the hang-out time after our Saturday night service. It is a pretty small role-but one that's easy for me to do and maintain because I enjoy it. What things that you naturally enjoy doing can you do to help others?

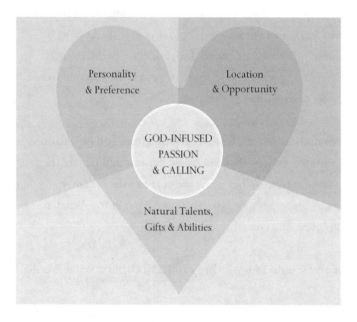

One of the healthiest things you can do while discovering and pursuing your passion is talk about it with a trusted group of friends. Don't be afraid to share and discuss your thoughts and dreams. Everyone has a passion, and while other people's passions are different from your own, that doesn't mean they can't appreciate yours. Talking about your passion will help you become more at peace with it, and discussing your ideas may end up opening doors and opportunities that you never imagined. Sure, every so often you'll stumble upon someone who will listen to your passion and look at you a little funny, but don't let them deter you from being honest with yourself and other people.

Stephanie, a twenty-three-year-old, admits, "I do not know what I want to do with my life. I can see myself doing many things, but I can't seem to find that one thing that is my passion . . . that thing that brings me joy and fulfillment. When I first began thinking about all this, I freaked out. However, in the past couple months God has really given me a peace about it. I really feel like he is working in my life right now to develop my passion, whatever it may be."

Stephanie says she is beginning to realize that God isn't as concerned with what she does as much as with how she does it. "I can see myself doing many things," she says, "but if I am not doing them joyfully and for God's glory, then there will never be fulfillment for me or for those who I come into contact with."

Though she used to be somewhat envious of people who always knew what they wanted to do and were passionate about it, she is growing more comfortable with the unknown.

"I wanted that so badly—to know I was on the right track, going in the right direction," she says. "However, the more I think about it, the more I like the not knowing. It is exciting! It forces me to give more over to God—to surrender my thoughts, plans, everything! I think the more I feel I don't know, the more I know God knows—does that make sense? It is a reassuring feeling. I am not going to say that there is never frustration or anxiety in the unknown, but it is encouraging for me to know that God has a purpose for my life and if I am daily striving to know him and live for him, he will show me in his perfect timing."

Stephanie reminds herself frequently that God sees the bigger picture; he is the artist with the paintbrush. "All I see are the individual strokes he is making, but what I can't see is how the whole picture looks," she says. "I have grown to trust that what he has in mind is a beautiful picture and I am part of it."

MYTH BUSTERS: THE TRUTH ABOUT FOLLOWING YOUR PASSION

Once you identify your passion and begin pursuing it, everything will be perfect, right? Quiz time!

True or False: **If You Follow Your Passion, Then the Money Will Follow.**

False. It is commonly said that if you follow your passion, you will eventually make money doing what you love. While this is often the case, it is not always the case. Some people's passions and interests simply don't translate into a steady income. You may only be able to pursue your passion in your part-time or in your spare time. But that doesn't mean you should give up. One of my closest friends, Cindy, works collecting hospital records during the day, but in her free time she is busy pursuing her passion as a church planter. Her full-time paying job supports her desire to be involved in ministry.

If you have children, family responsibilities, or heavy debt, you may not be able to afford the time or resources to become a full-time songwriter, sculptor, or _____.

"I have many passions in life," says Sean, a thirty-year-old. "God has filled me with some of those; others are a result of my flesh and need to die. I love to rock climb, and I believe that is God-given. Does that mean I should quit my job and pursue rock climbing full-time? Not at all. I am a husband and a father, and as such I have responsibilities beyond myself. In fact, this year, as a new father, I am learning just how selfish I truly am. I still go rock climbing but just not as often as I used to. Some afternoons now require that I talk to my wife or play airplane with my little girl."

You may have to get creative in order to pursue your passion. Katie, a twenty-four-year-old, pursued a BA in performance for the French horn while attending college. "I wanted to play movie soundtracks, but then I realized that I would have to be one of the top three horn players in the world," she says. "By the time I was there, I would be sixty years old with arthritis in my left hand. Somewhere in the midst of my search for a grad school, I realized that I didn't have enough passion to go to school for two to three more years with the guarantee of getting out, taking twenty-five to fifty auditions against two hundred other French horn players all with the hopes of getting a twenty-thousand-dollars-a- year job, and teaching lessons with all my free time in order to make it work."

Since graduating from college, Katie hasn't played the horn once. Instead, she is focusing on writing and recording her own songs.

"I have always been a poet and musician," she says. "Isn't being a singer/songwriter the next logical choice? It is my true passion. I am sure of that. I have done everything within my power to independently pursue my passion, including being crazy enough to record and release an album from scratch and start a grassroots record label."

In order to make her passion a reality, Katie works as a full-time shift manager at Starbucks, where she earns a steady income and health benefits to support her music habit.

It may take a while to get to the point where you can do what you love even part-time. It may require years of school-ing or working two jobs. It may require adapting to a lower-cost lifestyle. But if you truly love what you do, then it will be worth it.

True or False: **If You Follow Your Passion, You Will Enjoy All of Your Work.**

False. If you decide to pursue your passion as a business oppor-tunity, you are going to be stretched and challenged. Some of the work is going to be difficult and not a lot of fun. You may be a fabulous artist, but managing the business side of the operation may be a real challenge.

Even when you do what you love, there are still trying moments when you'll be tempted to quit. Turning your passion into a part-time or full-time job is challenging, and you may discover that you lose some of your passion when it becomes your work.

Some passions invite us out of our normal comfort zone. You may feel passionate about working with disadvantaged kids, even though you grew up in a well-to-do home. Or you may want to help people in a third-world country even though you can't speak their language. Pursuing a passion that God has placed in your heart doesn't mean it won't stretch you.

Responding to a passion will also challenge your motives for doing things. You may love music and have a gift for singing, but that can easily be twisted into something that glorifies you rather than God. Someone who thinks they deserve to sing all the solos obviously needs a reality check. Someone who carries secret pride about what they do, even though in public they give all credit to God, needs to look at their motives. It all goes back to Psalm 37:4: "Delight yourself in the LORD and he will give you the desires of your heart." Gifts from God are meant to be used for him. Being gifted with a skill and ability should result in greater humility, not a greater pride in yourself.

The fact that you have a passion for something doesn't mean that desire is meant to rule you; your passions are always subject to the Cross. When placed in the context of living out the Christian life, these passions are designed to be used to put a smile on God's face (which is a simple way of saying to glorify him).

True or False: If You Follow Your Passion, Your Response to It Will Never Change.

False. You may do the same thing day in and day out for the next sixty years. But then again, you may not. Life is filled with changing seasons. Your response to a passion will change depending on all kinds of factors, including your age, location, maturity, marital status, financial status, parental status, the age of your children, and other family needs. There will be times when you will be able to pursue your passion whole-heartedly with abandon, and other times when you will have to put your desires in the backseat to deal with more pressing concerns or needs.

Susan, a forty-eight-year-old, says she always dreamed of working with exotic animals. While attending college, where she majored in art and elementary education, Susan worked at a local zoo. After graduation, she worked as a school-teacher for six months before realizing the profession wasn't for her. Susan decided to become a flight attendant.

A number of years later the two jobs merged when an ex-zookeeper invited Susan to work her "cats" at school assemblies. "On my off days from flying I would clean their dens, cut up deer carcasses for freezing, assist in walking the tiger, lion, and cougar, and pet them!" Susan says. "Dream fulfilled."

As Susan's heart, interests, and life have changed, God has used it all to fulfill her dreams.

This is one quiz you may have been glad to fail! Don't be discouraged. The truth is, following your passion will not always be easy. That doesn't mean it's not rewarding beyond anything money can buy.

LEARNING TO FLY

Several years ago, one of my twentysomething male friends met someone. He was clearly falling head over heels, and he had that gushy, dazed look of being in love written all over his face. When I asked him about the girl, he said something I have never forgotten. After describing her beauty and personality, he concluded, "She just makes me fly inside."

I smile every time I think about that expression. And it's a phrase I now use to describe my passion. Writing makes me fly inside. When I sit down to write, I feel the holy hum of God's presence. There are days when writing is truly a spiritual experience that awakens the very fibers of my being as I do what I was created to do. This isn't something that just writers experience; anyone who has responded to the passion that God placed inside of them can know this feeling. I've listened to people from different walks of life—from scientists to psychologists to maintenance personnel—describe their work in the same way: They are living out a response to the passion that burns inside of them. Their work is something they can't *not* do, either.

My friend Robert Jobe, a filmmaker, producer, actor, and musician (as well as the son of Spanish missionaries), had a profound dream that illustrated the importance of recognizing and pursuing your passion. He describes walking into a packed auditorium. He arrived late and took an open seat next to a man and his son.

Robert introduced himself to the man by saying, "Hi! Who are you?"

The man turned to Robert and said, "I'm Carlos and I'm a carpenter."

"You misunderstood my question," Robert said. "Who are you?"

"I'm Carlos and I'm a carpenter," the man repeated.

Robert asked Carlos the same question several more times before he grew frustrated.

"I don't think you understood my question," Robert explained. "What is your passion?"

Carlos looked directly at Robert and welled up with tears. "My passion is painting. That's my passion."

"Then, Carlos, you're an artist," Robert said.

The tears began to flow.

"I want you to say that you're an artist, Carlos."

In a barely audible voice, Carlos said, "I am an artist."

Robert asked Carlos to say it again and again and again.

By the end of the dream, Carlos was standing on top of his chair yelling, "I'm an artist!" in front of an entire auditorium.

Robert woke up. Reflecting on his dream, he says, "I felt like God used this dream to show me that there are so many people who let their jobs define them, when there is so much more to them as individuals. I felt like the nine-year-old son in the dream represented Carlos's responsibility as a father. And that's why he does his carpentry, but his passion and the thing

God placed in his heart was to capture through painting the things that he sees with his eyes. I could imagine Carlos putting his son to bed and then gingerly walking up to the attic—the room filled with his canvases—to paint. It wasn't important whether or not Carlos was a professional artist. It just mattered that he painted, because that was the thing that set him free and made him human, even though he couldn't do it full-time. When he painted, it was like, *This is why I was born.*"

TAKING THE RISK

Pursuing your passion and getting to the point where you can fly can be rather turbulent. People who pursue their passion have to take risks. Many of them live on the edge—personally, relationally, and financially.

Hurtling down an icy chute at eighty miles an hour without a harness or any protection but a helmet isn't my idea of a good time, but for Anne Abernathy it's a way of life. Nicknamed "Grandma Luge," she is the oldest woman to compete in the Winter Olympics.

Anne's adventures in pursuing her passion began at the age of twenty-eight, during a ski trip to Lake Placid. Anne and a few friends wanted to see the bobsled run and noted a sign pointing toward the luge. "I didn't even know how to pronounce it," she says. "I read it as 'loogie.'"

One of the coaches, watching from over the wall of the track, asked if anyone wanted to try a luge run. "There were twenty people and eighteen took a step back," Anne says. "I took a step forward."

Anne reflects that after the trip "the sport laid on my heart for two years, and I couldn't shake it. I couldn't get it out of my mind." She finally began training full-time while still maintaining a full work schedule. At thirty-three, Anne qualified for the 1988 Calgary Olympic Games as a representative of the Virgin Islands. She was the oldest luge competitor. When one of her coaches realized her age, he promptly told her, "You are too old to luge."

"I wasn't five minutes ago," she quipped back.

Over the last seventeen years, Anne has proven that she still isn't too old. In addition to battling cancer three times during her athletic career, she has had a series of injuries that have resulted in thirteen knee surgeries, shoulder surgery, and wrist surgery. In January 2001, she had a severe crash that left her unconscious at the bottom of the run for twenty minutes with a closed head injury. Doctors told Anne that she would have seizures and be on medication for the rest of her life. She refused to take no for an answer and entered into aggressive physical and mental therapy.

Anne set her sights on qualifying for the 2002 Olympic Winter Games. "I was so focused that when I was actually checking in at the Olympic Village, it suddenly hit me that I had made it to the games but I might end up placing last," Anne recalls. "I began thinking, *Lord, why am I here, when I could be last?*"

At one of the computer kiosks in the Olympic Village, Anne's coach and doctor noticed a factoid that read, "Anne Abernathy, 'Grandma Luge,' oldest woman to compete in the Olympic Games."

"I thought, *God, is that why you have me here?*" Anne remembers. "When I went out to the luge track the next day, there
were people lining the track with signs that said, 'Go, Go
Grandma.' After the second day of competition, it took
nearly two hours to sign all the autographs from mothers
and grandmothers and people in wheelchairs who said, 'If
you can do this, then I can do anything.' It is not why I
thought I would go to the Olympics, but I was reaching people I didn't think I'd ever reach."

I caught up with Anne three days before Christmas in
2004. She was in San Antonio, Texas, taking a four-day break
before continuing the second half of the five-month World
Cup training and racing circuit.

"What most people don't realize is that the majority of
athletes are self-funded, particularly from the smaller nations
and even in the United States until you get to a certain level,"
she says, candid about her struggles. "I'm a five-time Olympic
athlete, and I am still unsponsored. I am trying to figure out
today how I'm going to live. I have a World Cup race on New
Year's Day, and I'm trying to figure out who to call to stay
with because I can't afford a hotel or car rental."

Other than a few skiers and skaters with major endorse-
ment contracts, most athletes, including Anne, compete for
the love of the sport. "There are no millionaire lugers," Anne
says. "It is tough. I am competing against athletes who train
full-time and are fully sponsored. Meanwhile, I have to pay
twenty to thirty dollars every time I take a practice run down
the track."

In 2004, Anne says the challenges were particularly over-whelming. She was considering retirement from the sport when she received an invitation to speak at a Red Hat Society convention. "I got up to speak to this group of women over the age of fifty and realized that if I go to the 2006 Olympics, I will not only continue to break records for the oldest competitor and tie the record for the most Olympics competed in, but I will also become the first woman over fifty to compete. I'm not just representing my country, I'm also representing my generation."

Anne Abernathy is pursuing her passion and calling wholeheartedly, but the journey isn't without risk. She risks her body, finances, and well-being to do what she does. In fact, there isn't much Anne doesn't risk. Yet reflecting on her career, Anne doesn't mention the risk, but focuses on the reward. She says that the Lord has been with her every step of the way. In addition to handing out New Testaments from the International Bible Society that feature her testimony, Anne distributes a small card that fans ask her to sign. On the card is Psalm 63:6-7, which reads, "On my bed I remember you; I think of you through the watches of the night. Because you are my help, I sing in the shadow of your wings."

"I have overcome so much to be a luge athlete, and I couldn't have overcome without the Lord being with me every step of the way," Anne says. "While I'm going through it, I'm not always sure he is there, but looking back I see him there."[2]

While most people don't have to endure the enormous risks that accompany screaming down an icy course on a sixty-three-pound metal device, risk is a normal part of life—especially for individuals who are willing to pursue their passion. Anyone who has ever started a new business, made an investment, stepped on stage, displayed their work, or mailed in an application has taken a risk. They risk financial loss, rejection, and failure.

FOUR WAYS TO CONVINCE YOURSELF NEVER TO TAKE THE RISK

1. Magnify the risk. Rather than focus on personal growth or success, focus on the risk. Calculate just how much risk you'll have to take and double it in your mind. The more you look at the risk, the less likely you'll be to take it.

2. Go it alone. Don't ask for support or wisdom from others. And whatever you do, don't ask for prayer support during this time. Convince yourself that you are a lone ranger and no one could possibly help you. It is a surefire way to avoid risk altogether.

3. Discount the reward. Make a list of the pros and cons. Tear the sheet in half and throw away all the pros. Avoid the bright side at all costs. It will make you want to find a happy place in the dark somewhere.

4. Don't trust God. Even if God has made it abundantly clear that he's calling you to do something and proven himself faithful in the past, avoid being obedient. Instead, choose to do your own thing and play it safe. You'll not only minimize risk, you'll limit your personal growth and ability to glorify him.

Yet when we take a risk—especially one that evolves from trusting God or being obedient to him—we are given an incredible opportunity to grow. Learning to fly is risky business. Crash landings usually hurt, and it's hard to get up, brush yourself off, and try again. Stepping out and doing what you were created to do rather than what is expected of you is hard. Even faith is a risk, so living a life of following Jesus is littered with risk.

There are so many people who have mistakenly given up on their passion because life hasn't gone the way they expected or thought it should go. As a result they have quenched the embers of the passion within their hearts. Yet God invites us to take a risk and allow the embers to come back to life. Any step—even a small, incremental step—can allow your passion to reignite.

God wants us to live in a posture where our hands are open and extended, not clinging to the things of this world. He designed us to live openhanded lives so that the passions we possess don't possess us. I have a little picture in my mind of God handing me a large diamond. If I hold the diamond too tightly, it becomes like glass and is able to cut and deform my hand. But if I hold it with an open hand, there is no way it can hurt me, and I'm able to share the beauty of the diamond with others.

The openhanded lifestyle is risky. People might take things from us, hurt us, or belittle us. But Jesus asks us to take the risk, and to show us how, he took it himself by laying down his own life. He demonstrated what an openhanded life looks like and how it can glorify God. As Ephesians 5:1-2 encourages, "Be imitators of God, therefore, as dearly loved children and live a life of love, just as Christ loved us and gave himself up for us as a fragrant offering and sacrifice to God."

I recently stumbled upon a powerful question on some online message boards: What would you do if you knew you could not fail?

Think about that for a second. What would you do? Make a list below.

_____

_____

_____

_____

_____

I have strained my brain on that question for some time. My first thoughts were about buying a winning lottery ticket, applying to Harvard, and competing in the Olympics. Then the thoughts became a little more altruistic. I'd search for a cure for cancer or AIDS, start a ministry of orphanages around the world, or help alleviate third-world debt.

But as I thought a little more, I realized that a life without risk would be a life without God. If I can do everything on my own and be sure of the outcome, then I don't need God. I merely exist. And what a sad existence that would be. Without the potential for failure, there isn't the thrill of success. The journey becomes a long, straightforward drive through

Kansas rather than a twisting, challenging adventure through the Rocky Mountains of Colorado.

The willingness to risk and take a chance that you might fail is actually a gift. It gives depth and texture to life, and more importantly, it allows us to grow in our trusting relationship with God.

LIVING COURAGEOUS LIVES

Good films have a way of going beyond entertainment; they permeate your soul. They challenge you to step up to the plate of greatness. The epic film *Braveheart* is a bold invitation to fight for what is right despite personal sacrifice. *Radio* is a compelling reminder of the life-changing power of compassion.

Why are these films captivating? Because they awaken something inside our hearts; they invite us to live courageous lives.

If you are going to pursue the passion that God has placed in your heart, you will need courage—maybe even more than you realized. It takes courage to take the first step. It takes courage to take risks. It takes courage to do something new. And it takes courage to make a difference.

Maybe that's one reason Jesus told his disciples on several occasions, "Take courage!" Consider the moment when Jesus was approaching his disciples in the middle of the storm. At first glance, they thought Jesus was a ghost. Jesus' response was memorable: "Take courage! It is I. Don't be afraid" (Matthew 14:27). Later, before his crucifixion, Jesus encouraged his disciples, "I have told you these things, so that in me you may have peace. In this world you will have trouble. But take heart! I have overcome the world" (John 16:33).

The disciples desperately needed courage, and Jesus reminded them how to find it. He recognized that courage is an act of the will. You don't just stumble upon it.

> Courage requires the belief that something greater than yourself is at stake. It also asks you to trust that Someone greater is at work.

One of my favorite verses in the Bible is Isaiah 43:1-3: "This is what the LORD says—he who created you, O Jacob, he who formed you, O Israel: 'Fear not, for I have redeemed you; I have summoned you by name; you are mine. When you pass through the waters, I will be with you; and when you pass through the rivers, they will not sweep over you. When you walk through the fire, you will not be burned; the flames will not set you ablaze. For I am the LORD, your God, the Holy One of Israel, your Savior.'"

As you pursue your passion, remember that wherever you go, God goes before you. In Revelation 22:13, Jesus says, "I am the Alpha and the Omega, the First and the Last, the Beginning and the End." There is nowhere you will go that God has not already been.

Risk is a healthy part of life. But the good news is that you don't have to face any risk alone. God is with you. And isn't a little risk worthwhile if it means you get to fly?

Are You an Intro or an Extro?

Knowing who you are—including your strengths and weaknesses—
is essential to determining what type of work environment is best for
you. Check the statements below that best describe you.

○ You enjoy attending lots of
social functions.

○ You get your energy and
ideas from being around
others.

○ You've been described as
the life of the party.

○ You live your life as an open
book.

○ You love being the center
of attention.

○ You fill your social calendar
with events six or seven
nights a week.

○ You tend to act and then
think.

○ You require downtime on
a regular basis.

○ You find that sometimes
you just need to get away
by yourself.

○ You need a quiet office
to work.

○ You appreciate a degree
of privacy.

○ You enjoy sitting back and
watching other people
interact.

○ You prefer a social
calendar with two to four
events a week.

○ You tend to think and
then act.

If the majority of your marks are in the left-hand column, then you're
probably an extrovert. People energize you. Interacting with others
improves your work performance and challenges you to go above
and beyond in what you do. You're likely to be most successful in
an environment that requires contact with the public. Whether you're
involved in sales, management, or working with clients directly,
you're naturally going to thrive in a workplace that maximizes your
contact with others.

If the majority of your marks are in the right-hand column, then you're probably an introvert. You enjoy working with other people, but you definitely need your space and some downtime. You're likely to be most successful in an environment that has limited contact with the public. Now that doesn't mean 100 percent of your time will be spent alone in your office tackling the next big project, but you'll probably find yourself a little more comfortable taking a role in the administrative side of the business.

If your marks are evenly spread between the two columns, then you have a balance of introverted and extroverted qualities. You are energized when you're with people, but you also enjoy taking some time to be by yourself. Be aware that you may be more introverted or extroverted during different seasons of life. With that reality in mind, you'll find yourself not only comfortable but successful in a variety of work environments.

Innovation:

Where Does It Begin?

Live so that the preacher doesn't have to make stuff up at your funeral.

Unknown

While many people make art, it takes a true innovator to create his own art form. Keith Gibson's artistic journey began with a simple desire to make something beautiful out of other people's leftovers. He started with a pile of plastic grocery bags and used packing material and masking tape to create a basic form. Then he glued pieces of broken glass onto the form to create a crystal-like design.

As he continued working, Keith discovered that glass was easier and safer to work with if it was heated to soften the sharp edges. He set up a lab of sorts in his garage and began working with different colors and types of glass—everything from beer bottles to broken car windows. Eventually Keith learned that if he took a glass bottle, heated it in an oven, and then covered it with silicone, he could use professional scissors to actually cut the bottle into strips so he didn't have to glue pieces of glass onto a form one by one.

Keith's imagination and artwork took flight. He built castles and birds and flowers and seashells. Friends and neighbors began taking note of his extraordinary work. Some offered to buy his pieces, but he refused, noting that his art was simply a gift from God that he wanted to share with others.

One evening, a friend casually joked that he thought it would be great to have a giant, lifelike T. rex poking its head through the ceiling of his living room. Keith didn't take it as a joke; he took it as a challenge. Months later, Keith announced to his friend that his T. rex was ready. The friend had forgotten about the conversation but quickly remembered when he saw the fifteen-foot-tall dinosaur head.

Taking one look at the spectacular piece, the friend remarked, "It's absolutely amazing, but my wife would kill me! This is too good to keep."

Today, the T. rex decorates the children's section of the local library.

As an innovative artist, Keith has a vision that stretches beyond creating beauty—he wants to give beauty away. He recently created a life-size glass sculpture of an American eagle holding an olive branch in its talons. Keith felt led to send it to the president of the United States as a gift to one of our nation's enemies. He believes it is a tangible way to fulfill Jesus' call to bless our enemies. Through a series of circumstances and connections, the eagle arrived at the White House and awaits being sent out.

Keith describes his artwork as something he is compelled to do. "At times, when I'm creating, I can feel the hair on the back of my neck stand up," he says. "It's like I can feel the very presence of God."[1]

Anyone who knows Keith will tell you he's deeply spiritual, highly creative, and refreshingly innovative. To support his artwork, wife, and child, he works as a full-time medic.

Pursuing his passion hasn't always made Keith's life easy, but it has made it beautiful. He has found a way to blend his calling to promote peace, reconciliation, and healing with his passion to create art, and the result is innovation.

CALLING + PASSION = **INNOVATION**

Anyone can do a job. Anyone can do ministry. How you infuse your passion into what you are called to do is what makes you unique. That's the seed of innovation. And that is why it's so important to not just be obedient to your calling but also to pursue the passion in your heart.

People who combine their calling and passion cannot help but be innovative. They cannot help but be individuals who transform their communities and their world.

DON'T SKIP THIS

Don't skip this just because it looks a little unusual! Believe it or not, you can read it! Aoccdrnig to rscheearch by Cmabrigde Uinervtisy, it deosn't mttaer waht oredr the ltteers of a wrod are in; the olny iprmoatnt tihng is taht the frist and lsat ltteer be in the rghit pclae. The rset can be a taotl mses and you can sitll raed it wouthit a porbelm. Tihs is bcuseae the huamn mnid deos not raed ervey lteter by istlef, but the wrod as a wlohe. Amzanig, yaeh? Dno't eevr be arfiad to be inonatvie. You can do aamizng tnghis wehn you put yuor mnid to it.

(Adapted from http://homesteadingtoday.com/vb/archive/index.php/t-75725)

For some, calling and passion are very much the same thing. My friend Wendy doesn't just feel called to teach, she is passionate about it. She teaches algebra and calculus in a low-income area because she wants to make a difference. At twenty-seven years old, she was recognized as Teacher of the Year for her school district.

While her heart breaks for the students who drop out of school because of pregnancy, drug use, and alcoholism, she celebrates with the students who graduate and go on to college. She recently had a particularly difficult student who approached her at the end of the year and said, "Ms. Wendy, I know I haven't been easy. I haven't done my homework, and I don't get this math stuff very well, but the way you treat me, the way you respond to me, it's like I look in your eyes and I see Jesus looking back at me."

Comments like that keep Wendy going. She recently wrote a federal grant that awarded her school 1.7 million dollars for programs, and she's currently managing the funds to improve her local school system.

Other people find creative ways to pursue their calling and passion simultaneously, like Kenny Mitchell, a church planter in New York City who feels called to full-time ministry but has a passion for music. In addition to growing and nurturing a congregation, he works as a DJ in some of the hottest night clubs not only in Manhattan but around the world. Kenny has been able to share his faith with countless people who would never darken the door of a church, and he serves as a lifeline for spiritual renewal to members of the community.

in·no·va·tion (ˌi-nə-ˈvā-shən) *n.*

The introduction of something new.[2]

You may be more of an innovator than you realize. When you introduce a new concept to your workplace, you're an innovator. When you seek to restructure, create efficiency, or think outside the box, you're an innovator. When you breathe hope, life, and encouragement into a situation, you're an innovator. Your unique presence can transform the attitude, atmosphere, and vision of the place you work.

Several years ago, I discovered that the head of the ski school where I worked was a Christian man who was responding to the calling on his life and passion in his heart. While he didn't openly talk about his faith with anyone who wasn't a Christian, his values and beliefs were quietly displayed in the ski school's policies and the way he managed the staff. The turnover rate among employees was incredibly low, and morale was surprisingly high.

Every fall the ski school held its tryouts for new ski instructors, and more than a hundred people would apply for a handful of slots. What fascinated me most about the process was the director's attitude. He made it very clear to everyone involved that he was more interested in hiring great people than great skiers. "I can teach anyone who is willing to become a great skier," he said. "But not everyone is willing to become a great person."

As a result, the ski school didn't always have the fastest, hottest skiers on staff, but it had the best people, and this resulted in some extraordinarily high customer-satisfaction ratings. In fact, under the director's leadership, the ski school was consistently ranked as one of the best in the country. Less than a year after he accepted a job with a different company, the ski school was no longer on the list.

Sometimes your mere presence in a situation—the subtle differences in the way you do things from the way anyone else does—makes all the difference.

As you respond to the question, *What the heck am I going to do with my life?* the passion that resides in your heart, and the calling on your life, you can't help but live a transformational life. It's a life marked not just by the constant change and growth that is taking place in your own soul but also by the impact you have on those around you.

> When you have the courage to pursue the unique blend of calling and passion that you have been given, you are going to stand out as an agent of hope, a source of inspiration, and a reminder to others that there is more to this life.

Being an innovator may never make you rich. Or powerful. Or even well-known. In fact, the vast majority of people who pursue their passions are unknown—except in the families and communities where they have become agents of change. Consider the moms and dads who combine their calling to be parents with their passion for raising great kids. Local store owners who blend their businesses with a passion for treating their employees well. Artists who simply for the joy of the art create new works that never make an appearance in galleries or museums, but still manage to invoke life, hope, and wonder in the few who see them.

The world is full of innovators who use their callings and passions to help others. Take Brittany and Robbie Berquist—only fourteen and twelve years old—who founded Cell Phones for Soldiers, collecting old cell phones and selling them to companies that refurbish them for resale. In nine months, their effort resulted in more than $250,000 worth of prepaid calling cards, which enabled American soldiers in Iraq, Afghanistan, and Kuwait to call home.

Or the Reverend Cecil L. "Chip" Murray, who twenty-seven years ago joined the small First AME Church in Los Angeles as pastor. Even as he retires, his exhortations to his congregants to take the high road and fulfill their responsibility to those less fortunate continue to transform the congregation and community.[3]

Or Shane, a twentysomething who in 1998 decided to pursue her dream of making films in Hollywood. In 2000, she cofounded Sodium Entertainment, and she recently returned from Africa, where she helped film a documentary to raise awareness about the AIDS crisis.

Or Hans and Susan Oines, a young couple involved in residence life at a college in Alaska because they are passionate about college students and feel called to make a difference in their lives.

They are all everyday people living out their callings and passions in the best ways they know how and transforming the world around them as only they can. But it's far too easy to read about such people and do nothing. This is not about them. It's about you. What one-of-a-kind blend of passions, desires, and calling has God placed in your heart?

Describe your passion.

_____

_____

Describe your calling.

_____

_____

Record some ideas on how you can fuse your passion and calling. Is there something new God is calling you to do?

_____

_____

What is stopping you from pursuing that place of innovation in your own life?

WHY ME?

In Exodus 4, you'll find the story of a humble man named Moses. At this point in his life, his calling to lead God's people and his passion to see them set free from the tyranny of Egyptian rule are fused in a life-altering encounter with God.

But Moses is plagued with self-doubt. He asks, "Why me?"

Yet God remains patient and gracious in his response. He

gives Moses the exact words to say to the Israelites and promises to be with him every step of the way. Still Moses objects. In essence, Moses is battling it out with God over the very thing God created him to do. Moses offers a laundry list of objections, and God answers every one. But Moses still cries out, "Lord, please! Send anyone else" (Exodus 4:13, NLT).

At that point the Bible makes a small but significant observation: God got angry with Moses. Now, God still answered Moses' concerns—even allowing his brother, Aaron, to serve as a spokesman—but he got mad. And I wonder if there are times we laundry-list him with all the buts . . .

> but the student loans
> but I don't know them
> but I don't know how
> but I don't like school
> but I've never been there
> but I'm not good with words
> but I don't believe in myself
> but my parents wouldn't approve
> but my friends would never understand
> but I don't know where to begin
> but I . . .

. . . and he gets a little miffed or at least a bit tired of our excuses, our self-doubts, and our God-doubts—refusing to trust and begin the innovative life he's called us to.

So what is stopping you from taking the next step?

Have you ever considered how your individual personality can help you discover the right career? Consider the following traits:

Realistic

Personal characteristics: genuine, stable, shy, persistent
Sample occupations: mechanical engineer, drill press operator, aircraft mechanic, dry cleaner, waitress

Enterprising

Personal characteristics: adventurous, ambitious, self-confident, energetic, domineering
Sample occupations: real estate agent, entrepreneur, market analyst, attorney, personnel manager

Investigative

Personal characteristics: analytical, independent, introverted, cautious, curious
Sample occupations: surgeon, physicist, economist, actuary, electrical engineer

Social

Personal characteristics: cooperative, generous, sociable, helpful, understanding
Sample occupations: interviewer, history teacher, counselor, social worker, clergy

Conventional

Personal characteristics: efficient, practical, calm, conscientious
Sample occupations: CPA, typist, file clerk, teller

Artistic

Personal characteristics: imaginative, idealistic, disorderly, impulsive, emotional
Sample occupations: interior decorator, drama teacher, advertising manager, journalist, architect*

*Adapted from Career Management by Jeffrey H. Greenhaus (Chicago: The Dryden Press, 1987). Used with permission.

Reality:

Why Is This So Hard?

Do what fulfills you. I have friends who worked all of their lives doing something they didn't enjoy because there was security in what they did, but they never enjoyed anything they did. If you have to work, you might as well enjoy it, and you'll live a lot longer if you have some fun with it.

Dois I. Rosser Jr., age eighty-three

A few years ago, I stumbled upon a little book called *The God Who Hung on the Cross* by Dois I. Rosser Jr. and Ellen Vaughn. The book tells miraculous stories of God's work around the world through a businessman and a bedridden pastor. I had to know more.

So I called Mr. Rosser.

It turns out that Dois I. Rosser Jr. was born in the eastern Blue Ridge Mountains of Virginia in the middle of the Great Depression. When he was five years old, his family moved to Hampton, Virginia. Rosser's dad earned only thirty-five dollars a week as an engineer at a nearby shipyard. A vegetable garden and a cow helped put enough food on the table for the family. "We didn't have anything," Rosser says. "But we didn't know it, either. Our home was always open to all."

In a small country church, at the age of twelve, Rosser accepted Christ. "I always felt that God was with me, even though I did a lot of things I'm sure he didn't approve of," Rosser recalls.

After graduating from high school and attending a small business college, Rosser enlisted in the United States Air Force. He served two years and two months during World War II. After the war, he and a partner started an insurance and real estate company. Rosser added an automobile dealership and began fixing up houses on the side. His businesses continued to grow over the years. He bought out his partner and eventually owned a number of companies that he rolled into the Pomoco Group, a holding company.

Even though he served as a Presbyterian layman, Rosser says he lived as if his professional life and his spiritual life were two different worlds. It wasn't until he heard the teaching of a pastor named Dick Woodward that he realized the two worlds were meant to be one. "As I listened to Dick teach, I realized that if you are really a follower of Christ, then you don't make decisions outside of your relationship with him," Rosser says. "It is like a marriage. I try not to make any decision without talking to my wife or at least considering her well-being in the decision-making process."

Rosser was so impacted by Woodward's teaching that he felt compelled to share it. He partnered with a few others to put the teaching on audio- or videotape. "We thought we could do it for twenty-five-thousand dollars over a six-month period, but it took a lot more [money] than that, and two years later we finally had it on tape," he says.

As Rosser learned more about broadcasting, he discovered an odd phenomenon. Because of the transmitting strength of international radio stations, he could broadcast Woodward's teaching to almost 450 million people around the world for the same price as transmitting the message locally.

Rosser began broadcasting the messages in Central and South America. A few years later, he was contacted by a young Chinese man who asked if he could broadcast in his native country, opening the door for the messages to reach more than nine hundred million Mandarin-speaking Chinese.

On a trip to India to look at broadcasting opportunities, Rosser learned through a chance conversation with a minister that it only cost five thousand dollars to build a local church. Rosser couldn't believe it required so little. He began paying for churches to be built. Eventually others contributed to the work.

As of December 2004, International Cooperating Ministries (ICM), a ministry of the Rosser Family Foundation, had built over 1,600 churches around the world and had 280 more under construction. The daily broadcasts of Dick Woodward's messages have a potential listening audience of almost four billion people in twenty-four nations.

And even though Dick Woodward is bedridden with severe spinal deterioration, he works six to eight hours a day preparing topical sermonettes based on Scripture. "He can't even go to the bathroom on his own or brush a fly off his nose," Rosser says, "but he has still been able to put together more than 760 fifteen-minute programs with the use of a voice-operated computer."

At eighty-three years old, Rosser sounds like a teenager

whenever he talks about the ministry or what God is doing in his life. He can barely contain his enthusiasm, and he's quick to give God all the recognition.

But he's also willing to admit that it wasn't always easy. "When I went into business, I started with five hundred dollars," he recalls. "I borrowed thirty thousand dollars and later I told the banker that I wouldn't have loaned it to myself. It is easy to talk about the winners, but there were also losers. We didn't start at top speed; we had to grow. For twenty-plus years everything we had was mortgaged to the hilt."

Some of his businesses took a greater toll on his life and family than others. "If there was a real time of struggle, it was with the car business—which is a tough business. It took a terrible toll . . . long hours, customer satisfaction, detail-based . . . and it is a very small percentage of profit despite what people think. . . . It required an enormous input of time and energy."

Rosser is quick to point out that there is a price for every job, and it is important to know the price. "For a lot of people it is wishful thinking; they'd like to do something, but they never really try and they are not willing to pay the price. It is easy to look at people who have done well and think that success starts at ground zero, but that's not the case. I used to have a guy who would frequently say, 'Rosser is the luckiest man I know.' A friend who finally responded to the guy said, 'It is amazing how lucky Rosser gets the harder he works.'"[1]

When I reflect on Dois Rosser's story, I'm reminded of how easy it is to fall into the trap of thinking that life comes easily to successful people. If you just read the corporate reports, you might think that Rosser was raised in a wealthy family or inherited his businesses. You could assume that he had a Midas touch when it came to business and all of his ventures turned to gold. It's tempting to think that it came easily and was relatively stress free, when in fact Rosser's story is filled with obstacles and challenges.

No matter what you do—whether you are trying to raise children or build an international corporation—success, by its very nature, demands time, sacrifice, and hard work. Starting a business, entering a new profession, going back to graduate school, raising a family—these are not easy ventures.

Every dream comes with some not-so-glamorous realities. Some are easy to spot, and others take years to discover. As you consider *What the heck am I going to do with my life?* keep in mind this reality check.

CHALLENGE .0001

On several occasions, I have gotten together with girlfriends and taken one of those last-minute, rock-bottom-priced, all-inclusive vacations to Mexico. I've traveled to Puerto Vallarta, Cabo San Lucas, and most recently, the Mayan Riviera with my husband, Leif. The quality of the resorts—including food, bedding, services, and staff—differed with each resort's rating (two stars qualifying as "sometimes scary" and five stars qualifying as "usually wonderful"), but the basic amenities were the same. There were different restaurants to choose from, including buffets with some strange and mysterious entrées. There were large pools with countless chairs for tanning, and there were always a few salespeople nearby ready to sell you everything from timeshares to silver (or not-so-silver) jewelry.

But some of my favorite parts of an all-inclusive resort are the activities and events. There's usually a team of activity coordinators that hang out near the pool and offer everything from water basketball and water polo to dance lessons, cooking lessons, and shows during the evening to make sure you are fully entertained. Think summer camp for adults.

At first glance these resort employees—who are getting paid to play water volleyball and teach a lighthearted aqua aerobics class—seem to have the best jobs in the resort. They're basically paid to laugh, play, and have a good time while encouraging others to do the same. Meanwhile, the other employees are cleaning rooms, cooking, serving food, and doing a lot of even less-enjoyable tasks. It didn't take me long to figure out that if there was one job for me at the resort, I'd definitely sign up to be an activity coordinator.

But one night, Leif and I had a chance to talk to an activity-team member. It was 9 P.M. and he was encouraging us to come to the evening show. He was dressed in a Mayan outfit as part of the theme and still bubbling with the same energy and enthusiasm we had seen him display in the pool at noon.

"I bet there are a lot of people who would love to have your job," I said encouragingly.

"You are right," he replied. "Lots of people would look at this job and think it is the best. But the reality is that most of them wouldn't last more than a few hours."

Before I knew it, he was off inviting another group of people to attend the show. But something in his words stuck with me. Over the remaining three days at the resort, I saw the men and women coordinating the activities in a different light. I noticed their quiet frustration when, despite countless attempts, no one would participate. I watched as one young woman who had coordinated a game of water volleyball found herself in an uncomfortable situation with one of the male guests, who had drunk one too many *cervezas*. She played it off as a joke, but the fear mixed into her expression was obvious. Most of all, I noticed the high-energy pace and positive attitude they kept up all day—something I couldn't fake or stimulate with all the caffeine in the world. And I realized that maybe working at the activities center isn't the best job at the resort.

> Reality: Your dream job may not be such a dream after all.

The fact is, there are hundreds if not thousands of jobs that sound like really good ideas. They sound fun. They sound rewarding. Some even sound dreamy. But in reality, they all have negative aspects. Maybe they don't pay well. Maybe they ask you to give more than you have. Maybe they demand a certain attitude that you just can't maintain. Maybe they're good for a season or two, and then you burn out. And maybe there are downsides, negative sides, and even dark sides to the job that you never thought of. There is no perfect job.

CHALLENGE .0002

Judy Woodruff, a veteran of broadcast journalism who joined CNN in 1993, once observed, "It takes another journalist to understand the peculiar highs and lows of this field. Some days you feel like you've had the greatest ego massage; then the next day you've been trampled on."

Schoolteachers enjoy the summers off, but the school year is hectic and demanding. Doctors and surgeons earn high salaries but work long hours and often live on call. Flight attendants enjoy the benefits of travel privileges, but they earn them with miserable shifts for the first few years as they begin the long climb toward seniority. Accountants enjoy a steady demand for their work, but the spring tax season can be highly stressful and rather . . . taxing. Working in child care seems like a dream, until you remember that cold and flu season tends to hit young ones (and their caretakers) hard. Waitresses can make great money, except there are always going to be slow shifts and cranky customers.

Reality: Every job comes with a unique list of pros and cons.

You'll never know the highs and lows of a job until you do it. You can have either a high-paying job or a carefree job, but it is nearly impossible to find a job that promises both. And it's even harder to find one that delivers on that promise.

After moving to Steamboat Springs, Colorado, in 1987, my mother studied for her real estate license. She began working in someone else's office, and a few years later she opened her own. She became extremely successful, but the success didn't come without a cost.

As a real estate agent, my mom was constantly on call. If a client had a whim to look at property, she was ready to show it to them. The problem was that clients called all the time. Literally. They called during family dinners and holidays. They called on weekdays and weekends. When they forgot which time zone we were in, they called at 2 A.M.

It is easy to look at the situation and think that my mom just had boundary issues. But anyone who has been in real estate very long knows that if you are going to build a successful real estate business, you can't build very many boundaries. Success demands that you be available.

Every business has its own drawbacks, and it is important to do some research into whatever profession you are considering. Talk to people who hold your dream job and talk to the people who work for them. Pick up the local phone book or go online and select a few companies you think you'd like to work for. Visit their human resources office. Ask your friends and neighbors if anyone they know is in that line of work. You'd be amazed at how many people are willing to talk frankly and honestly about what they do. While you can't know everything about a job until you actually do it, you can still have a pretty good idea of the pros and cons before signing any contracts or going back to school.

Problems are inevitable no matter what job you choose. Every job has its issues, and you are going to need wisdom and grace to handle them. You are going to need faith, patience, and character to handle them well. You can't check your faith at the door of your workplace. It is one of the places you will need God the most. So remember that while problems are inevitable, through prayer you don't have to tackle them on your own.

WHAT'S IMPORTANT TO YOU?

When it comes to the workplace, everyone has different values and priorities. Spend the next few minutes ranking these twelve areas in order of importance when it comes to your work:

___ Personal Growth

___ High Salary

___ Great Benefits

___ Flexibility

___ Vacation Time

___ Competition

___ Great Coworkers

___ Great Boss

___ Enjoyable Work

___ Making a Difference in People's Lives

___ Job Security

___ Opportunity for Promotion

Circle your top five priorities. Put a line through your bottom five priorities. What's truly important to you in a workplace?

Michael Jordan knows how to get air. Big air. He played an amazing 41,011 minutes in 1,072 games and finished his career with 32,292 points, 5,633 assists, and 6,672 rebounds. Jordan was a five-time NBA Most Valuable Player, ten-time All-NBA First Team selection, and one of the "50 Greatest Players in NBA History."[2]

Without question, Jordan's got game. In the wake of a successful career, he has been asked to endorse, promote, and release a long list of products. One that recently caught my eye in a magazine article was Michael Jordan Daily Condition Shampoo. It comes in a hip orange bottle with a black cap and is priced under eight dollars. You might be tempted to pick up the celebrity shampoo except for one little detail: Michael Jordan is bald.

While I'm willing to trust Jordan for big air, I'm a little less confident in his ability with big hair.

> ### Reality: You are not good at everything.

The shampoo discovery reminded me that we all have our limits. I'd love to tell you that anything is possible, but the truth is you were created with specific strengths and weaknesses. That was not a mistake. Too many people foolishly spend time thinking, *If only I could.* But that time is wasted. You need to come to terms with the fact that God has something better suited for you.

If you find yourself exhausted and spent from your work rather than engaged and satisfied, you may be working outside your natural abilities. Whether by choice or by assignment, you may find yourself working in an area that you just aren't suited for. With a lot of extra hours, you may be able to do the work required by your boss, but it's difficult and at times grueling. That doesn't mean that you can't do the work—even for another twenty years or more—but you'll find it a struggle to enjoy what you do. You may be able to stick it out, but it's important to weigh the cost of staying with something you don't enjoy against the risk and potential benefits of pursuing a different line of work.

Don't despise your lack of talent or your inability to do something. I can wish all day that I could sing like Josh Groban, but it is not going to happen. By coming to terms with what you can't do, you can discover what you were meant to do.

At the same time, it is important to remember that each of your strengths has a parallel weakness. In other words, what makes you good at something will make you not as good at something else. For example, if you are naturally artsy and creative, you are less likely to be well-organized. If you are naturally relaxed and laid-back, you probably struggle to maintain any sort of rigid schedule. These are broad generalizations, but no matter what your strength is, keep an eye out for its accompanying weakness.

WHERE ARE YOUR SKILLS?

You are uniquely wired! You bring certain talents and skills to any organization, workplace, or entrepreneurial endeavor. Circle the number that best correlates with your feelings about each statement below, using this scale: 1 = Not at all, 3 = Rarely, 5 = Occasionally, 7 = Often, 9 = Definitely.

1. I enjoy working with people.

1   3   5   7   9

2. I can easily connect lessons, facts, or statistics to draw appropriate conclusions.

1   3   5   7   9

3. I can identify the source of a problem pretty quickly.

1   3   5   7   9

4. I can think abstractly.

1   3   5   7   9

5. I can predict how people are going to respond.

1   3   5   7   9

6. I'm interested in the cause-and-effect relationships in work.

1   3   5   7   9

7. People naturally like my ideas and the way I present them.

1   3   5   7   9

8. I can predict roadblocks before they become an issue.

1   3   5   7   9

9. I enjoy figuring out how things work.

1   3   5   7   9

10. I like to find the optimal solution to a given problem.

1   3   5   7   9

11. People have described me as a visionary.

1   3   5   7   9

12. I am a naturally good communicator.

1   3   5   7   9

13. I enjoy wrestling with ideas, concepts, and theories.

1   3   5   7   9

14. People ask me to help with problems at work.

1   3   5   7   9

15. I tend to look at the details of a given problem.

1   3   5   7   9

16. I find it easy to motivate people in a positive way.

1   3   5   7   9

17. I prefer to focus on the big picture.

1   3   5   7   9

18. I have good people skills.

1   3   5   7   9

A. Add up your responses to questions 1, 5, 7, 12, 16, and 18.
TOTAL _____

B. Add up your responses to questions 2, 4, 8, 11, 13, and 17.
TOTAL _____

C. Add up your responses to questions 3, 6, 9, 10, 14, and 15.
TOTAL _____

In which category did you score highest?

A: This reflects your interpersonal skills or how well you are able to motivate, communicate, and relate to others. You manage people well and have good working relationships.

B: Your responses reflect your conceptual skills or how well you are able to see the big picture. You can see where a company or product is going and generally how to get there.

C: Your responses reveal your diagnostic skills or ability to understand the relationships between cause and effect, service and satisfaction, or quality and sales. You can usually identify the cause of a specific problem and suggest a solution.

You probably have a blend of all three skill sets, but identifying your strengths and weaknesses can show you where you can be an asset and where you need the help of others in your work.[3]

CHALLENGE .0004

Charles Williams made his living as a building contractor, but his true passion was cooking. When he opened a hardware store in California, shoppers quickly noted the immediate extension of his excitement: an unusually fine collection of European cooking utensils. In 1958, Charles moved his store to downtown San Francisco, where women who lunched in nearby restaurants were amazed by his selection. Twenty years later, he found a buyer who was willing to take the chain national, so Charles could focus on the actual cooking products. You may recognize the store: Williams-Sonoma. Today, the billion-dollar empire includes brands such as Pottery Barn, West Elm, and Hold Everything.

> Reality: You have to start somewhere.

Every great career has a starting point, and it is usually near the bottom of the corporate ladder—not at the top or even on a middle rung. If you know the right person or have the right work experience on your résumé, then you may be able to start a rung or two higher than the next newbie, but you are still going to be toward the bottom unless you are simply changing ladders.

One of the biggest struggles many people face starting out is a sense of entitlement. The thinking goes something like this: *I walked out of my parents' house, and I should be able to walk into one just like it right out of college.* It is easy to forget that it took two or three decades of saving, sacrifice, and hard work for your parents to get where they are today.

MARGARET FEINBERG

The same mind-set follows people into the workforce. The salary should be higher. The promotions should come faster. The office should be bigger (or you should have an office).

Underneath the sense of entitlement is the compounding idea *I should be further along by now because of* (fill in the blank with *my parents, my education, my background,* etc.). Yet developing work skills and relationships with your clients and coworkers takes time. Very few people were truly overnight success stories. The vast majority worked hard and put in long hours for years in order to get where they are today. Even in their impatience to get things done, they were still patient about obtaining their overall goal.

You do have to start somewhere, but with a humble attitude and the right perspective, just the chance to try is a privilege. And eventually—maybe not today or tomorrow or even the next day, but one day—you will move up.

CHALLENGE .0005

If you've been raised with a strong belief in the American Dream, you may think that through sheer willpower and hard work, the world can be your oyster. Yet is this dream consistent with reality? Does everyone really have the same opportunities?

Abraham Lincoln is regarded as one of our nation's greatest presidents, but few realize the challenges he faced securing the office. Consider his track record:

1831   Business failure
1832   Defeated for legislature

1833	Second failure in business
1834	Elected to legislature
1835	Fiancée died
1836	Mental breakdown
1838	Defeated for speaker
1840	Defeated for elector
1843	Defeated for land officer
1843	Defeated for Congress
1846	Elected to Congress
1848	Defeated for Congress
1855	Defeated for Senate
1856	Defeated for vice president
1858	Defeated for Senate
1860	Elected president

Lincoln was familiar with failure and self-doubt.

> Reality: Not all doors will immediately open for you.

"Often our culture acts as if all doors are wide open to everyone," says Betsy Taylor, a counseling psychologist in Winston-Salem, North Carolina. "Just think of the timeworn phrase, 'Anybody can grow up to be president of the United States.' Maybe one day that will actually be true. But we have a way to go. Class, gender, language, race, ability, and disability . . . all can play a role in terms of who may have connections, who may be supported and nurtured in their life/career development, and who may be overlooked or even blocked in their growth. I think we are moving in the right direction, but we also need to help young people learn to anticipate challenges and obstacles and how to deal with them."

Taylor also believes that we need a broader definition of success. "Physicians, attorneys, and corporate executives are important in our culture, and certainly we want to assure access to everyone. But realistically, not everyone will have the grades, the LSAT scores, or the funding to gain entry to and get through law school. Nor should these goals necessarily be considered the ideal."

Taylor has talked with quite a few graduate and professional school students who realize with dismay halfway through their classes that they have little interest in what they're learning, or what their futures are likely to offer them, yet they are so deeply mired in debt that they decide to finish and work in the field to pay off their loans. "And what message are we sending to young people who want to enter the professions, but who may not have the credentials to do so?" she asks. "Are the 'proper' credentials the successful outcome of a liberal arts education? And what of high school students who for various reasons find it difficult to go to college or choose other training options? Their career pathways are even more devalued by our culture, certainly in terms of the huge disparities in earning potential and also in social status."[4]

CHALLENGE .0006

As a twentysomething, Anne taught music in an elementary school before taking an eight-to-five job as a claims adjuster

Everyone has a way in which they best process new information. Your learning style isn't just important when you're taking classes; it's also important in your workplace as you learn about the job as well as teach and instruct fellow employees. Which of the following learning styles describes you best?

Eyes Wide Open Learner. You learn best when information is presented using visual aids and tools. In school, you may have preferred instructors who used PowerPoint presentations, movies, or other images to note the key points of the lecture. You tend to notice details—whether it's in film, art, or the design of a room. You tend to notice not just how something is written but the design of the message. When presented with new information, you prefer to sit back and watch before jumping in. You're not afraid to ask someone to show you how something is done. You don't hesitate to open a textbook or workbook in order to deepen your understanding of key concepts. And when you think about something you've learned, you often have a mental picture of the material.

Rough 'N Tumble Learner. While all learning is an active process, you learn best when you're able to experience a new concept firsthand. You learn more by doing than by listening or watching. If possible, you prefer a hands-on experience. While textbooks and lessons are tools, you'd much prefer being in a laboratory setting where you can be physically active and engaged in the learning process. You may learn best when you're sitting in the front of the classroom, where there's less distraction, and you're able to use materials—whether it's a three-by-five card, Excel spreadsheet, or model—to help you learn. Sometimes abstract concepts are a little tough for you to grasp right away, but if someone will turn the learning process into an activity, you will remember it forever and be able to communicate it clearly to others.

All Ears Learner. You've probably been described as a good listener. You learn new concepts by listening to someone else explain them. You prefer straightforward presentations and lectures followed by an interactive discussion. If you haven't done it already, you really want to buy a tape recorder to track important details and thoughts. You love your iPod. You enjoy audiobooks. You are particularly attuned to the way things sound. You're naturally drawn to certain singers, speakers, and voices. And when you have a problem, you find that sometimes just talking about it reveals the perfect solution.

While you may be a blend of two or even all three of these learning styles, there's probably one that predominantly describes you. It's important to recognize how you learn so you can grasp new concepts in your workplace.

for an insurance company. She describes the job as "incredibly unfulfilling" but accepted the position in order to make ends meet. "Hating my job with a passion forced me to examine what I really want to do with my life," she says. "When I examined myself and implored God to give me hints at my calling, it became exceptionally clear that I needed to go to seminary. I knew I had to be incredibly serious about it, or my soul would just wither and die from lack of passion. I couldn't be more excited."

> Reality: It is normal to experience frustrations in trying to find your niche.

Even people who know what they are going to do with their lives still have to figure out the details. You may try something new and discover you don't like it. It is okay to change your mind. Very few people do one thing for their entire lives. Be patient. So often our lives are based on our own timing instead of God's.

Polly, a twenty-nine-year-old, says she has discovered that some things—like a relationship with God—need to be priorities, and when that happens everything else seems to fall into place. "I think it is entirely possible that in some cases . . . we just grow into where we are meant to be. I think it is that way with me. I work on what I have been given and follow my heart and where I believe God is leading me and *boom*— suddenly I realize this is it. All our childhoods we can't wait to reach each milestone, but if I let myself think that way,

1. Medical assistant

2. Network systems and data communications analyst

3. Physician's assistant

4. Social and human service assistant

5. Home health aide

6. Medical records and health information technician

7. Physical therapist aide

8. Computer software engineer, applications

9. Computer software engineer, systems software

10. Physical therapist assistant

Based on projections from the Bureau of Labor Statistics 2002–2012.
http://stats.bls.gov/news.release/ecopro.t04.htm/.

how much joy and fulfillment will I miss out on? I guess what I'm doing right now is trusting that even though my interests are across the map and I may not be sure that what I'm doing now is permanent, that God will let me know when the time is right."

CHALLENGE .0007

Several years ago, I stumbled upon a great ad in a Christian magazine. At the top it read, "God loves you and has a wonderful plan for your life." Below the caption was a serene picture of a beach chair and a large umbrella resting at the center of a crescent-shaped white-sand beach overlooking some of the most beautiful turquoise water in the world. Underneath the picture it said, "Unfortunately, this probably isn't it."

> Reality: Success demands sacrifice, hard work, and perseverance.

The ad contains far too much truth. We expect life, even life with God, to turn out one way, and instead it dumps us on our heads. Like a Six Flags roller coaster, it is filled with highs and lows, sudden curves, and the occasional loop-d-loop. Even if you have a strong faith, being successful at your job will be tough.

You can dream about your passion all day long, but eventually you have to do something about it. If you are going to be successful or skilled in what you do, then you are going to have to work hard and stick with it.

At the age of five, Danny Clayton became fascinated with the people he heard on the radio. A few years later, he told his dad that he wanted to be a disc jockey. "He told me that most DJ's need second jobs," Danny recalls. "I somehow had the presence of mind to tell him that Wally Phillips, a huge Chicago radio personality, didn't have a second job."

Danny attended college and worked part-time as a disc jockey. "It was a tough business when I turned pro during my junior year of college—it is even tougher now, but I worked hard and was patient," he says. "It amazes me to count the number of people I used to work with who are no longer in the business."

At age forty-four, Danny says he has only had two jobs in his life: paperboy and DJ. One lasted a year and a half, and the other almost three decades. "I truly believe that deep down every person knows what they want to do but is afraid to admit or expose what that might be," he says. "Realizing that the climb is long and hard is important, and it sure makes the thin, hungry years not as bad, but when you truly like what you do, it sure makes it a lot easier to get up in the morning."

Perseverance makes an enormous difference—sometimes all the difference—between those who succeed and those who don't.

CHALLENGE .0008

One of my favorite moments in the classic children's tale *Alice in Wonderland* comes at a point when Alice arrives at a crossroads. She notices Cheshire Cat in a nearby tree and asks for advice as to which road she should take.

The cat promptly asks her, "Where do you want to go?"

"I don't know," she admits.

"Then, any road will take you there," the cat responds.

Cheshire Cat's answer is unexpectedly profound. Knowing where you want to end up has a tremendous impact on the decisions you make along the way. When you choose one path, you eliminate another.

> Reality: For every door that opens another has to shut.

This is one of the most challenging realities of life. It is easy to think that anything is possible, but inherently when you make a choice to go in one direction, you have to say no to another. Some rare individuals are able to earn a law degree, get their MBA, and become a doctor all by the age of forty, but for most people the kind of time and money required to do it all just isn't reasonable.

Alyssa, a twenty-five-year-old, says that she has been struck by the reality that there is just not enough time to do everything she wants to do. "As I was growing up, there was a real feeling of idealism in the air, especially toward girls. I was told that I could do anything I wanted," she says. "That's true to some extent, but no one ever told me that I can't do all of it at the same time."

There's going to be an issue of missed opportunities. No matter how hard you work to keep every door open, there are some that close without your permission. "I'm sure it sounds funny to say it, but to some extent I think I became disillusioned by the real world because there are so many *or's* that you have to choose between," Alyssa says. "Ballerina and professional tennis player, for example, are totally out of the question at this point. The bottom line is that it is really hard to make choices, and it is a million times harder with the self-inflicted pressure of comparison, whether to your own ideals or to other people's. I have been working on giving myself permission for life to work out differently than I initially planned it."

CHALLENGE .0009

A young boy stumbled across an old man carving into the side of a mountain. Next to the man he could see other carvings, many of which were hard to identify. Each looked like some kind of form, but whether it was an animal or human or object he could not tell. Other carvings were more recognizable. He stared at a carving of harvest time that had never come to fruition. He ran his hand across the mane of what he guessed was a lion. He recognized the beginnings of a large tree.

With boldness the boy approached the old man and studied his work. At first, he didn't recognize the carving. But as he looked closer, he saw the man's detailed work in the rock. He was carving the image of a beautiful woman. Though the carving was seemingly perfect in design, the man was still working.

"Do you know her?" the boy asked bravely.

"She was my wife," said the man, unwilling to look up from his work.

"When will you be done?"

"Love has no end," the man answered. And he continued his work until the day he died.

> Reality: People who love what they do will naturally work longer and harder.

The importance of doing what you love cannot be overstated. When you do what you love to do, you naturally come alive as an individual. You have renewed enthusiasm and vigor for the task at hand. You can work longer, harder, and more readily. Enjoying your work is like a secret fuel that keeps you going. If you like what you're doing, you'll inherently have the energy to keep going even after others around you have run out of gas.

COMING TO TERMS

No matter what the inkling, compelling, calling, or passion in your life, it all begins with the first steps. Prayer. Research. A job application. Taking a few courses. Volunteering. Working part-time. Whatever is resounding in your heart, you are going to have to start somewhere. You are going to have to work hard, make sacrifices, learn from your mistakes, and all the while rely on God.

Sure, you can avoid the realities of pursuing your passion, but it will require giving up your passion—and that's a high price to pay. Far too many people spend their whole lives thinking that after they retire and the kids are in college, they'll begin to do what they feel compelled to do. In many cases, that time never comes. Why wait?

5.3 Reasons Not to Burn Bridges When You Leave a Job

1. Life is full of surprises—including the most surprising of all: You just may need that job back one day!

2. Even if you never want to work for *that* place again, you still might need a recommendation from someone who works there.

3. The trivia game Six Degrees of Kevin Bacon challenges players to connect any film actor to Kevin Bacon through actors they've shared movies with. For example, Elvis Presley was in *Change of Habit* (1969) with Edward Asner, and Edward Asner was in *JFK* (1991) with Kevin Bacon. Therefore Elvis Presley has a Bacon Number of 2.* The idea that the world is really a small place holds true today. So leave your job on good terms—even if your boss doesn't know Kevin Bacon. You'll be better off.

4. When you leave a job on bad terms, you're just setting yourself up to stew over the issues for weeks, months, and possibly years to come. It's much better to draw the line now, let it go, and cling to the good memories (or single memory if there is one).

5. The two most important days for making a good impression are the day you arrive and the day you leave. Make the last better than the first.

5.3. In case no one has told you before, you're better than that.

*Taken from http://en.wikipedia.org/wiki/Six_Degrees_of_Kevin_Bacon/.

.0007

Impact:

Will It Live beyond You?

A lot of people are waiting for Martin Luther King or Mahatma Gandhi to come back—
but they are gone. We are it. It is up to us. It is up to you.

Marian Wright Edelman

Last year I was on a rather bumpy flight from Seattle to Dallas-Fort Worth. As we approached the airport, the captain announced that because of stormy weather, the plane was being rerouted to land at a military base more than a hundred miles from DFW. Once we touched down, we discovered that for security reasons, none of the passengers would be allowed to exit the plane.

My husband and I sat on the plane—which was filled to capacity—for more than two hours, waiting for the weather to clear in Dallas-Fort Worth. As time passed, the passengers grew increasingly restless and hungry. After more than an hour, the stewardess announced that food would be served. It turned out that the captain of the plane had gone to a nearby McDonald's and purchased enough cheeseburgers and fish and chicken sandwiches to feed everyone on our plane. He paid for the food out of his own pocket, knowing that he wouldn't be reimbursed. But his thoughtful act went one step further: He also purchased enough sandwiches for everyone on the airplane parked next to ours!

This faceless American Airlines pilot committed a simple

act of kindness that I will never forget. He went above and beyond the call of duty and helped make a difficult trip more comfortable through his generosity. Whether or not the pilot was a Christian, I do not know, but his act certainly demonstrated Christlikeness. And it made an impact that lasted a lot longer than memories of typical flights that weren't delayed—which I honestly don't remember much about.

The desire to make an impact is significant. While some people describe the desire as increasing around the midpoint of their lives, many young adults want to make an impact at an early age.

At twenty-one, Brian Mosley picked up a book designed for forty- and fifty-year-olds called *Halftime: Changing Your Game Plan from Success to Significance*. The author, Bob Buford, examines how the first half of life—often earmarked by "getting and gaining, learning and earning" and striving for success—compares to the second half, which should be about regaining control and discovering God's desire "for you to serve him just by being who you are, by using what he gave you to work with."[1]

Brian says that when he finished the book, he thought, *Good for Bob and that generation. I hope I never experience what he did.* "In other words, I didn't want to get to forty-five or fifty-five or sixty-five and wonder how to make the last half of my life significant," Brian says. "I want to live significantly now."

Many in their twenties and thirties feel the same way. They don't want to wait until the second half of life to begin making a difference. "There seems to be a hunger to make an impact as soon as you can in life," Brian adds. "It is almost like there is the obligation to make an impact somehow during the span of your life, and it is better to get a jump start and go for it early. Part of this hunger, I believe, is driven by the idea of a valuable life. How can I live a life that is valuable and not just self-serving?"

Brian decided to do more than just talk about making an impact. During college, he joined his family on a trip to Africa that changed his life.

"Those four weeks [in Tanzania] were one of the most pivotal moments in my life," he says. "The first ten days we spent traveling to Magambua and documenting the lives of these missionaries. I never realized that missionaries weren't all pastors. In fact, there was a single girl teaching the missionary kids; a man who was good at building things who moved his family over to help keep things running for the other missionary families; a Swiss-German family there to be the first ever to create a written alphabet for the tribal language, Sandawe; another single girl there as a nurse; and finally an associate pastor from Pennsylvania who moved his wife and three kids over to help start a church in the village. Talk about living out your faith."

The experience left Brian with one burning question: "God, what other opportunities are out there for me to use my video and communication skills to serve you?"

Brian contacted more than forty mission agencies, explaining his interest. Packets of information began pouring in. "The agencies didn't want to personally respond," Brian recalls. "They just wanted to push paper back and forth. Out of all my inquiries, there was one couple that responded with a personal e-mail. A few months later they were visiting our town and sat down at dinner with [my wife] and I. There in a Black-eyed Pea [restaurant] they answered questions and shared of their years of experience in Africa. It was just what I needed—personal interaction."

Brian realized that there were countless others who had a similar need, and in 2000 he founded Rightnow to serve as a connecting point between people looking for ways to serve overseas and the organizations that provide the opportunities. Rightnow is always looking for places to meet young adults eager to serve. In 2004 they launched a brand-new event called Fusion, designed to help twenty- and thirtysomethings find ways to fuse their faith and life. In addition to Fusion conferences, Rightnow has participated in a variety of concert, church, and campus-based events, including Passion conferences like OneDay 2000, Passion Experience 2001, Thirsty Conference 2002, OneDay03, and Passion 05.

Brian's story illustrates that everyone can have an impact. Everyone is capable of making a difference by using the passion and talent they've been given. But before that can happen, we have to get past the myths and misconceptions about having an impact that can hold us back.

MYTH #1: YOU HAVE TO BE MOTHER TERESA

Brian says that a lot of people think they have to be an expert, a genius, Mother Teresa, or Billy Graham to make an impact. "It is the group of people who think *I am worthless; how could I make an impact on anyone?"* Brian says. "It is fun to help people realize that their passion for motorcycles or design talent or sense of adventure or computer skills are God-given and can have an impact if you are willing to use what you've been given."

On the other side, in some cases it takes a very smart, experienced, strategic person to make the right kind of impact. "Not just any Joe Blow can go live in a tribal area creating the first written alphabet from a tribal language that has no written history," Brian says. "Sometimes people show up thinking that a willing heart is all they need to make an impact, but they really should be learning a trade or becoming knowledgeable in a certain field so they are more useful. I have seen this with college students who want to drop out so they can go and minister overseas or in the U.S. I think they are limiting their long-term options for impact when they choose to forsake learning and developing their craft or expertise just to go do it."

For Brian and the staff of Rightnow, helping individuals find the right opportunities to serve is a balancing act. It's a matter of encouraging people while reminding them that everyone is needed to serve, including those with less glorious positions. "Thinking of engineering a water well makes me want to phrase the question like this: Who is more valuable— the person who laid out the designs for the well or the person who dug up the dirt?" Brian explains, "I don't believe there is a correct answer. The tragedy is when the engineer settles for digging up dirt and the construction worker thinks he has nothing to offer and never pursues an opportunity to serve."[2]

> "The key to making an impact is finding the right place for your unique skills and passions to really thrive."   —Brian Mosley

MYTH #2: YOU HAVE TO DO IT FULL-TIME

There is a common misconception that you have to be involved full-time in a nonprofit group or ministry in order to make a difference. You don't have to wear a cleric's collar or have a master of divinity to reflect Christ. You can do it right where you are in your workplace.

The Bible is filled with people who weren't in full-time ministry but still used their professions and work to glorify God. Remember the innkeeper who provided a humble place for Jesus to be born. Consider Joseph of Arimathea, who paid for the place where the Son of God was buried. (Granted, it was a short-term investment.) The Bible tells of a man who provided the place and meal for the Last Supper. All these individuals were clearly used by God as they gave what they had to him.

As we read the Gospels, it becomes clear that Jesus wasn't concerned with what people did as much as how they did it. Zacchaeus, a tax collector, was never told to change professions, but rather to stay in the same line of work and do it honestly. The Roman soldier whose child was ill was commended for his faith, but Jesus never commented on his military occupation. And the entire Sermon on the Mount is focused on how we treat others, not our professions. Obviously, God is willing to use people in all types of work to glorify himself.

But this isn't just a New Testament phenomenon. Think of Esther, who became involved in politics and was placed in leadership for what the Bible calls "such a time as this" (Esther 4:14). And when God wanted to build the Tabernacle, he used all kinds of individuals with different talents and gifts.

Exodus 31:1-6 says:

Then the LORD said to Moses, "See, I have chosen Bezalel son of Uri, the son of Hur, of the tribe of Judah, and I have filled him with the Spirit of God, with skill, ability and knowledge in all kinds of crafts—to make artistic designs for work in gold, silver and bronze, to cut and set stones, to work in wood, and to engage in all kinds of craftsmanship. Moreover, I have appointed Oholiab son of Ahisamach, of the tribe of Dan, to help him. Also I have given skill to all the craftsmen to make everything I have commanded you."

God gave the workers the "skill, ability and knowledge" to create and design everything needed for the Tabernacle. Every worker was able to use his particular skill to make an impact by building the Tabernacle, a place of worship to God.

> As you seek to make an impact through your life, it is important to give others the time and space they need to make a difference too.

Give people room to be unique and different. 1 Corinthians 12:6 says, "God works in different ways, but it is the same God who does the work in all of us" (NLT).

Lisa, a twenty-three-year-old, decided to pursue her passion at a young age and started a successful photography business in high school. "I love photography because I can express emotions, ideas, and feelings. When I sit down to write, I get blocked off by too many ideas, but when a camera is in my hands, I become silent, and then I begin dreaming about what I want to do."

The vibrant twentysomething loves being exposed to new styles of photography and working on new projects. "One day I'm talking to a bride and groom; then five minutes later I'm planning trips to other states to photograph churches, while e-mailing friends about upcoming events and how my camera and I can help. There's nothing that compares to the reward and struggles of photography. It's always changing, and I love that."

Lisa has been able to take her passion and turn it into more than just a business—she uses it to make an impact. She has found a niche for creating stock photos for youth groups and churches. Lisa also travels to churches to help with their photography needs at a fraction of the normal cost.

MYTH #3: YOU HAVE TO DO SOMETHING BIG

Another misconception people have about making an impact is that you have to do something grandiose. A mission or outreach doesn't have to involve travel or have a global impact to change people's lives. Change happens at multiple levels—personal, community, state, national, and global. Every small initiative can make a tremendous difference.

Michael, a twenty-four-year-old, spent several years as a missionary before returning to the United States, where he currently works with the mentally challenged as an assisted-living worker. "I think about making an impact on the world probably about every day of my life," he says. "It affects everything I say and do. I try to make every opportunity count, and that's hard because in the place I work there is so much that I would like to say and do for the people, but 99 percent of them couldn't understand me anyway.

"It gets hard sometimes because I feel that because of their sicknesses, they aren't able to understand God and the grace of God, so I sometimes feel that doing another job would be better because I would be able to speak the truth to people that could understand," he continues. "On the other hand, I am able to take one of them to church, and he blesses me every Sunday while he has his hands raised worshipping and always makes me point him to the right Scripture even though he can't read. I also get to work with kids who have problems, some more severe than others, but I am able to see them change and become normal kids just through loving them. The reward might not be so visible, but I know God is working through me and in every step I take and every word I speak to them. Sometimes we won't see the fruit of what we do, but that shouldn't discourage us from doing what is good. It should motivate us to [work] harder."

WHAT MOTIVATES YOU?

Everyone is motivated differently. What makes you fly inside might make someone else crash. To make a lasting impact, you need to know what motivates you. Do you prefer to be managed or work on your own? What makes you want to work harder? Is it money? impact? verbal affirmation?

An interesting list of motivators was developed by H. A. Murray in the 1930s. Based on Murray's Manifest Needs, this list is designed to help you discover your motivational makeup.

Place checks by the categories that describe you best.

○ **Achievement.** You like setting goals and reaching them. You are willing to go the extra mile in your work. A little competition brings out the best in you.

○ **Affiliation.** You are a team player. You make friends with most people and enjoy healthy relationships at work.

○ **Aggression.** You sometimes start an argument just for the fun of it. You regularly become annoyed with your coworkers and have been known to carry a grudge.

○ **Autonomy.** You love your freedom. The less structure, the better. If too many restrictions are placed on you, there's a temptation to rebel.

○ **Exhibition.** You love being the center of attention. Whether it's through your humor, drama, or storytelling ability, you know how to capture an audience.

○ **Impulsivity.** You are spontaneous and openly speak your mind, but at times you look back and wish you had used discretion.

○ **Nurturance.** You look for ways to serve others and provide sympathy and comfort to those in need. You are known as a good friend, and you have a listening ear for anyone who needs it.

○ **Order.** You work best when your work area is clean and tidy. You avoid clutter and confusion. You enjoy systems that keep information organized.

○ **Power.** You enjoy leadership and assume that role in most situations. You often try to control your environment and influence those who are in direct contact with you.

○ **Understanding.** You enjoy learning and value logical thought and ideas, especially when they satisfy an intellectual curiosity.

Each of these areas can be a motivator in your workplace. Which best describe you? Which are currently motivating you? Which are you using to motivate others?

_____

_____

_____

_____

_____

_____

Betsy Taylor, director of the Pro Humanitate Center at Wake Forest University, believes it's important to think about the impact of your individual actions and capitalize on the opportunities that are before you to make a difference for others. It is essential to value contributions at every level and provide lots of support and encouragement for individuals to look for ways to effect change.

She notes that unfortunately, in our culture careers seem to be divided into "acquisitive" jobs and "giving-back" jobs. Yet within all professions, there are multiple opportunities to have a positive impact on the world. Taylor notes the following two qualities that are crucial for people to acquire:

Compassion: This includes not only a basic philosophy that we are all responsible to and for everyone on the planet, but also the idea that we should stay informed about what is happening in the world, who is in need, why, and what their lives are like physically, emotionally, economically, and culturally.

Integrity: This includes identifying and maintaining a set of values so that in our interactions with others, we act in ways that support those in need, across the board. Regardless of our profession, we seek out opportunities to express our basic values. This might involve offering pro bono services, serving on boards for nonprofit organizations, engaging in volunteer work, or creating community service programs.[3]

Your integrity will be challenged when your work and values collide. The word *integrity* is derived from the Latin *integra,* which implies wholeness or completeness. *Integra* is also the root word for *integer,* or whole numbers, and *integration.* As Dennis W. Bakke, author of *Joy at Work,* observes, "[Integrity] has to do with how things fit together in some cohesive and appropriate way. Being truthful is part of what it means to have integrity; living up to commitments is another."[4]

Have you ever stopped to think about the principles by which you want to live your life? What are your standards? It's easy to think about basic ethical standards, such as "I will not steal," "I will not cheat," or "I will not lie." But have you ever considered the specific standards you want to base your life and work on? Record some of the nonnegotiable principles of your life in the space below.

_____

_____

_____

_____

_____

Take some time to reflect on the Ten Commandments (Exodus 20) and the Sermon on the Mount (Matthew 5–7). Based on your reading of these passages and your notes from the previous question, record your own Top Ten Principles for Business.

1. _____

2. _____

3. _____

4. _____

5. _____

6. _____

7. _____

8. _____

9. _____

10. _____

Compassion and integrity can transform a workplace. Dwight "Ike" Reighard worked as a pastor for more than thirty years before reentering the corporate world when he was asked to be the chief people officer at Homebanc Mortgage in Atlanta, Georgia. "They asked if I could come shepherd their people," Reighard says. "I understood the word *shepherd* because that's what I have done as a pastor for all those years."

Reighard believes that you can turn an ordinary job into an extraordinary opportunity by realizing that God has placed you in your work to serve and influence others for his Kingdom. "You should find a company where your values and their values coincide," he says. "Find an organization that you're proud to say you're associated with. It doesn't have to be something exotic or sexy—as it has been said, there is just as much dignity in tilling a field as writing a poem."

If you're in constant conflict with your company's values, morals, or ethics, you're going to have a hard time making an impact. You'll also want to find a place that aligns with your talents and gifts. When you find a place where you're happy going to work, you are more likely to have an impact.

> It simply comes down to being like Jesus to the people you work with and for.

One of my close friends, Carol, is a full-time dental hygienist, but her gift is being used as a conduit of God's blessings. That may sound a little strange, but I have never met anyone who is so clearly used by God to provide for others on a regular basis. She is what Malcolm Gladwell, author of *The Tipping Point,* calls a "connector." Carol will have in her dental chair a single mom with a leaky roof she can't afford to fix, and two days later Carol will share the problem with a contractor who is in to have his teeth cleaned. Within a few weeks, the single mom's roof is fixed, the contractor has completed a kind and generous deed, and Carol has simply served as a vessel willing to connect the two.

You can make an impact wherever you are. No matter how big or small the title or pay, you can use your job and your relationships to glorify God and serve as a representative of his Kingdom here on earth. No gig is too small.

What's Your Natural Rhythm?

Whether you realize it or not, your life has a rhythm. There are times and seasons when you're more alert, awake, and active and others when you're more relaxed, restful, and subdued. When you recognize your own natural rhythm, you can look for or develop a work environment and schedule that maximizes your productivity and creativity. Don't wait for a manager to figure you out! Take the initiative and study your own productivity patterns.

Put a square around your most creative time of day. Circle your most productive time.

Midnight–6 A.M.   6 A.M.–noon   noon–6 P.M.   6 P.M.–midnight

Put a square around your least creative time of day. Circle your least productive time.

Midnight–6 A.M.   6 A.M.–noon   noon–6 P.M.   6 P.M.–midnight

Circle the workday that is the most creative and productive for you. Put a square around the day that is the least creative and productive.

Sunday   Monday   Tuesday   Wednesday   Thursday   Friday   Saturday

Rank your workdays from most creative and productive to least.

Sunday   Monday   Tuesday   Wednesday   Thursday   Friday   Saturday

Are there certain seasons or months that you're at your peak in creativity and productivity? Circle those months below.

January	May	September
February	June	October
March	July	November
April	August	December

Are there certain seasons or months that you are least likely to be creative and/or productive? Circle those months below.

January	May	September
February	June	October
March	July	November
April	August	December

Reflecting on the information above, when is the best time for you to start a new project? When is the worst time for you to start a new project?

Short-term project:

_____

_____

Long-term project:

_____

_____

What are the best days for you to work longer hours? What are the best days for you to go home early? When is the best time for you to take a vacation?

_____

_____

_____

What can you do to coordinate your personal and work responsibilities so you can maximize your natural rhythms?

_____

_____

_____

.0008

Balance:

Can You Hold It All Together?

There is no fun like work.

Dr. Charles Mayo, founder of the world-famous medical clinic

The film *The Incredibles* follows the story of a family of superheroes forced to live normal, anonymous lives after a series of lawsuits made the government hide them in the witness-protection program. Bob Parr, formerly known as Mr. Incredible, lives with his wife, Helen, formerly Elastigirl, and their children: invisibility-prone Violet, lightning-quick Dash, and baby Jack Jack. To protect their secret identities, Bob works as an insurance claims specialist, Helen acts like the perfect mom, and the three children are told to keep their superpowers to themselves.

But Bob can't resist the temptation to go back to his old life. When he is given the opportunity to be a hero, he jumps at the chance but finds himself in a trap set by an old nemesis. In the end, the whole family has to reveal themselves as superheroes in order to save their dad and the planet.

The film is a perfect blend of action, adventure, and comedy, but underneath the surface, *The Incredibles* touches on deeper issues of identity.

Rene Rodriguez, a reviewer for the *Miami Herald,* notes, "The underlying message in *The Incredibles* . . . is that we really *aren't* all created equal, that we should champion our own talents and peculiarities instead of trying so hard to fit in, and that to further mediocrity through conformity sabotages our potential as individuals (it's a theme shared by the *X-Men* pictures)."[1]

At one point in the movie, Elastigirl, aka Helen, tells her children, "Your identity is your most valuable possession."

Identity is one of the most precious characteristics of being human. Your identity is unique. Identity gives you context for life; it provides a foundation for how you interact with and respond to the world around you. That's why knowing your identity is essential.

Yet it's far too easy to allow what you do—whether it's a profession or a pastime—to define who you are as a person. Even if you can tag multiple degrees and awards to your job title, allowing what you do to determine who you are limits you to a one-dimensional life when you were designed for so much more.

> You are a living, breathing human being with feelings and emotions and relationships. You have highlights and lowlights; you experience thrilling moments and the mundane. You eat, sleep, and dream. You smile, laugh, and cry. And you are so much more than what takes place behind an office desk or in a cubicle.

Who am I? is one of the biggest questions we'll ever ask ourselves. It challenges our core beliefs—the foundations of who we are as individuals. Unfortunately, our society seems far more concerned with what we do. Think about the last time you attended a gathering with people you had never met before. After asking for your name and where you're from (if it's not obvious), most people will ask, "What do you do?" From your answer—whether you're working on Wall Street or you're between jobs—people will draw all kinds of conclusions about you. Over time some of these people will get to know you—the real you—but until then your occupation serves as a simple way to label or categorize you in people's minds.

It's not just when we meet new people that we allow our professions to define us. Our jobs can easily become the source of our identity. This happens for several reasons. For one thing, defining what you do is much easier than discovering who you really are. It's simpler to stick with shallow labels and generalizations rather than press into the depth of soul searching required for self-discovery. And it takes time to truly know yourself—your likes and dislikes, your passions and fears, your strengths and limitations. There usually isn't time in the transition between school and work for much discovery. You're immediately pigeonholed into a job or career, so you end up answering the question, *What do I do?* long before you ever have time to explore the question, *Who am I?* in depth. The result is that your profession overshadows your identity.

The danger in discovering what you want to do with your life before you figure out who you are as an individual is that you can become what you do. Kristie, a thirty-year-old veterinarian, has learned this lesson the hard way. She is convinced that what you do from nine to five does not determine who you are as a person. "That is a common mistake," she says. "One that I have made for my whole life. Now that I am a veterinarian, I realize that I could have worked in so many other ways to help animals and that veterinary medicine is only one possible option. Any other profession might have worked equally well for me, and I could have made animals my passion, hobby, or pastime. I would encourage people who can't figure out what they want to be when they grow up that being passionate about your hobbies can be as fulfilling as a good job—maybe even more."

One way to help separate what you do from who you are is to view your vocation and passion in broader terms. Instead of defining yourself as a third-grade teacher, recognize that your gift is teaching and that it's something you can use in countless professions. That way when you change jobs or enter a new stage of life, you are open to the different ways God can use you in a new environment. When you embrace a broad definition of what you do, the possibilities of using your talents and gifts expand exponentially.

But to figure out who you are and begin living in a way that is true to your identity, you need to find balance in your life. Balance is an issue everyone faces. A dichotomy is often made between work and living your life. Most people want a balanced and full life. They desire a challenging job that provides a good income, but they also want time for family, friends, service, and personal interests.

One clinical psychologist I interviewed noted that people seem to feel they have to choose entities. She observes, "It's

So where do you go to discover your true identity? You go to the One who made you. If you want to know who you are, then you need to discover whose you are. Ephesians 1:11-12 says, "It's in Christ that we find out who we are and what we are living for. Long before we first heard of Christ and got our hopes up, he had his eye on us, had designs on us for glorious living, part of the overall purpose he is working out in everything and everyone" ("The Message").

Consider some of the things God, your Creator, says about you in Scripture:

You are not only a child of God (John 1:12) but also an heir (Galatians 4:6-7). You are a new creation (2 Corinthians 5:17), a member of a royal priesthood, a holy nation, and a people for God's own possession (1 Peter 2:9-10). You are redeemed (Revelation 5:9).

You are chosen and appointed by Christ to bear his fruit (John 15:16). You are righteous and holy through Christ (Ephesians 4:24), a son or daughter of light and not of darkness (1 Thessalonians 5:5). You are a child of God, and you will resemble Christ when he returns (1 John 3:1-2).

You are no longer alone. You are a member of Christ's body (1 Corinthians 12:27). You are God's workmanship, his handiwork, born anew in Christ to do his work (Ephesians 2:10). You are called a friend of Christ (John 15:15).

You are a child of God, and that is the highest calling a person can have. Once that becomes part of your reality, you are free from having to be what the world tells you to be, and you can more fully become who God calls you to be. You can respond to the gifts and talents God has given you and recognize yourself as part of God's master plan.

likely a by-product of life in the twenty-first century—long hours in the office or factory have been supplanted by the possibility of limitless hours on the job via e-mail, voice mail, fax machines, and working from home. We can't even go on vacation without feeling guilty for not checking our palm pilots every few hours. And how many spreadsheets on laptop screens do you see on plane rides to Orlando or Cancun?"

C A R E E R   L I F E

The struggle is finding a balance between pursuing a career and having a healthy personal life and then maintaining that balance throughout different life stages. If you are starting a new venture—whether it is a new company or job—it is nearly impossible to balance everything because your work demands extra time and energy, extra hours to get ahead or keep up on projects, or extra work because you can't afford or find someone to do it for you. You may find yourself wrestling with the most basic limitation of them all: There are only twenty-four hours in a day, and in the end, you can only do what you can do.

Those first years of starting a new job, profession, or business are critical. You have to work hard and make sacrifices in order to succeed. It is like pulling back on a pendulum to get it started. It will bounce back and forth wildly at first, but slowly it will find an even, steady pace.

> Once you've overcome the initial hurdles that come with doing
> something new, you need to begin making choices that will allow
> you to find balance in your life.

The first step is coming to terms with the fact that you can
have what you want, but you can't have it all. You can't work
ninety hours a week and expect to have healthy relationships
with friends and family. At the end of the day, you are going
to be fried—emotionally and physically drained from all the
hours you put in at work. You need to determine what's
important to you and what steps you need to take to keep
those priorities in place.

If your friends and family are high priorities, then you'll
naturally want a job that is as close to forty hours a week as
possible. Jobs that require late nights or lots of travel usually
aren't conducive to building healthy relationships.

If your faith is a priority, then you are going to have to
make sacrifices and make time to grow spiritually. You may
need to wake up an hour earlier to spend more time in prayer.

If your hobby is a priority, then you may want to cut back
on some expenses in order to invest in what you love to do.
If you enjoy snowboarding, you may have to skimp on cable
television in order to buy a new board. If you are a movie buff,
you may decide to bring your lunch to work so you can spend
more cash on supporting your film habit. If you enjoy traveling, you may choose to work overtime and shop at second-
hand stores in order to underwrite your next adventure.

Once you recognize your top priorities, you can develop

strategies that will enable you to experience what is important to you. You may have to drive your car for another twenty thousand miles or give up two Frappuchinos a week, but change is possible.

List some of your top priorities below. What is truly important to you?

_____

_____

_____

_____

_____

_____

What changes do you need to make in your daily life to reflect those priorities? What changes do you need to make at work? in your finances? in your relationships?

_____

_____

_____

_____

_____

_____

Finding balance takes time and constant readjusting. What works for you in one situation may not work in another. As you seek to find balance in your life, here are a few things to consider.

MANAGE YOUR TIME

One of the most important skills you'll ever develop is time management. Everyone has areas where they tend to waste time. One of my biggest temptations is the television. Not only am I a reality-TV junkie, but I also love detective shows like *CSI*. I never wanted to grow up and become a couch potato, but after a long day's work, television is a fast and easy way to decompress. The problem is that it only takes a few shows until I'm hooked on a program. Then I need to watch the entire season of *The Biggest Loser* to find out who wins or watch the remaining episodes of *24* to find out what really happened. Before I know it, I am watching ten to fifteen hours of TV a week, which is equivalent to a part-time job. That time could be spent in so many more useful and meaningful ways.

Unfortunately, in front of the TV is not the only place where I tend to lose track of time. The Internet is another huge pitfall. I could spend an entire afternoon following all kinds of rabbit trails of information, and don't even get me started on eBay. Though I may learn a lot and discover a few deals along the way, I have to wonder if the time couldn't be spent better elsewhere.

Whether it is TV, the Internet, or some other time-sucking device, we all have areas of our lives where we could use our time more efficiently and effectively. Have you ever taken an inventory of your time? You might be surprised at where you're spending it. Consider recording where your hours are spent over a seven-day period. You may discover "free" hours that you could use for something better. For example, instead of watching two hours of television a night, invite friends over to hang out and play games. Instead of vegging out, you can build relationships. Or instead of checking your e-mail a dozen times a day, limit your Internet usage to once in the morning and once in the evening so you can give your energy and concentration to the people and events at hand.

You may be able to combine events to reflect your priorities. If you want to get in better shape and also reach out to others, you can go for a walk with a friend or neighbor. If you want to spend time with your kids and grow spiritually, then you may want to volunteer to teach Sunday school.

The reality is that it usually doesn't take a lot of rearranging, just a little creativity, to use your time more effectively.

REALIZE YOUR LIMITATIONS

You can help others; you just can't help everyone. Lyssie, a twenty-five-year-old, says, "I'm constantly tempted to do too much. The thing that helps me a little is to just think about how long life is and that God has a big plan which I can be a little part of. I don't have to change everything [or] right all the wrongs of the world. As my dad once told me, 'Stop trying to be the savior of the world. You are not qualified, and someone else is already doing it.'"

We are all called to serve others, but there are times we need to know our own limitations. Before you get involved in a situation, take time to pray. Check your motives. And

1. Avoid giving an immediate response. If you are prone to saying yes, then you need to buy yourself time to really consider the opportunity before responding. Rather than offer an immediate answer, have a standby answer such as "I need to check my calendar."

2. Ask if you can get back to the person the next day. Before you ever make any medium to major decision, sleep on it. This is just a piece of good old-fashioned practical wisdom. Most of the time—even in business—you can let the person know your response the next morning and it won't make a difference. Sleeping on a decision is a powerful tool. It buys you time to pray, seek wise counsel, and avoid the pitfalls of an emotional response.

3. Before you commit to an event or activity, ask questions about what it involves. You may assume the party is only going to last an hour or two, when it is designed to be an all-day event. You may think that volunteering to bring food to an activity is a onetime commitment, but you are really being asked to help for the next six months. Always clarify the details of what you are being asked before you make a decision.

4. If you are pressed to change your mind, restate your position calmly. If you said no once, say it again. If you are still pressed to say yes, gently remind the person that you've already decided to pass on the opportunity. Thank them for their time and quickly move on.

5. Remember that you have the right to say no. You simply can't do everything. If you are doing something out of guilt, you need to question whether you'd be better off not doing it at all.

remember that God is big enough to handle anything, with or without you.

Part of realizing your limitations is learning how to say no. I have been learning how to say no for as long as I can remember, and I still struggle to use that little word. It is so much easier to say yes to opportunities and events. If I don't keep an eye on my schedule, I can double- and even triple-book myself.

If you are going to live a balanced life and not spread yourself too thin, you need to learn to say no.

Another big part of realizing your limitations is learning to be content right where you are. Think short term. Far too many well-meaning teachers and professors have encouraged students to develop five- and ten-year plans. While these plans can be helpful for establishing goals and direction, it is important to remember that they aren't set in stone—and they're not going to happen overnight.

"So many people (including myself) worry about where they are going to be twenty years from now and don't live the life they are in," says Heather, a twenty-six-year-old. "It is great to plan and to have an education, but you have to be content with what you have now. A lot of the time people look to the future, and money is the first thing that pops in their head. I'm just realizing myself that there are so many more important things in life than the material things. I was once told that success is finding out what God's will is for you and then doing it. That is a great place to start."

FIND A HEALTHY ENVIRONMENT

The place you live is crucial to living a balanced life. Your home should be more than just a place where you store your stuff; it should be a place where you rest, reflect, and recharge your batteries. A place that calms your heart and soul. If you have young children or half a dozen roommates, creating a home that is a sanctuary may be challenging, but you should still search for an area of your house—whether it is a bedroom or balcony—where you can take time to sit still. It is in the stillness that you can more readily recognize the areas where you are out of balance.

Your work environment also plays a big role in your life. As you seek to balance your work life and personal life, step back and look at how your place of employment is affecting you. The environment you place yourself in—even at work—can have a huge impact on who you become. You may be in a healthy environment that challenges you personally, encourages you to use your talents, contributes to others, and causes you to grow as an individual. Your workplace may help you become a better person and know God more intimately. On the other hand, you may be in an environment that tears you apart inside, doesn't allow you to use your gifts, and brings out the worst in you. Bad work environments can promote backbiting, gossip, insecurity, and even depression.

Jen, a thirty-year-old with a college education, is currently working as a receptionist at an outdoor club in Lake Placid, New York. "I encourage people to stop and think about what type of environment they would like to be in," she says. "Someone who has just graduated college often labors over what to do with their life, but what's more important is deciding who you are. I don't mean to be cliché, but in real life people get run-of-the-mill jobs and find total fulfillment in who they are."

It's important to ask yourself where you would enjoy going to work every morning. If you are an introvert, you may enjoy a quiet job at a desk. If you are an extrovert, you may like working as part of a team. Do you want to be challenged in your work? Or do you prefer to cruise and use your energy and talent outside of work? Recognizing your personal needs will allow you to better evaluate your workplace and its impact on your life.

In order to restore balance to your life, you may need to switch jobs, go part-time, or take on less responsibility at work or church.

Signs That It's Time to Quit

— Your boss or fellow employees demean you. You are so verbally abused that you come home deflated.

— You are sexually harassed.

— You work sixty to eighty hours a week and the pay doesn't reward you for all the time. In other words, you may be making $40,000 a year, but if you are working eighty hours a week, that's like only making $20,000 a year for a forty-hour week.

— The stress is taking a toll on your health, relationships, and/or marriage.

— You can't think of one good thing about your job.

— You are bored to the point of becoming depressed.

Signs That You Need to Hang On to Your Job

— You recognize that you are in a healthy work environment.

— There are still a variety of training or promotion opportunities available
to you.

— The benefits package or pay is hard to beat.

— The job provides strong networking opportunities for the future.

— You don't have any peace about switching jobs at the moment.

— You realize that your situation is allowing you to grow.

Signs That You Might Be Fired Soon

— You are not included in meetings anymore.

— People begin whispering when you walk by.

— Your boss, secretary, and coworkers treat you differently. And it is not just
your imagination.

— You no longer get CC'd on e-mails or memos from your boss.

— A team of investigators just happens to be scheduled to visit the company
during your annual vacation.

Signs That You Are *Really* About to Be Fired

— Your computer is no longer on your desk.

— Security personnel appear shortly after you walk into the office.

— The key to your office no longer works.

— Your nameplate is suddenly missing.

— Your secretary or best friend at work recommends that you call in sick.

— Someone else is now using your office, cubicle, or workstation.

What You Can Do:

— Have a DTR with your boss. **D**efine **T**he **R**elationship with your workplace. What's working? What's not? What other opportunities inside and outside the company are available?

— Update your résumé.

— Expand your network.

— Trim your expenses.

— Put out feelers for a new job.

— Talk to family and friends.

— Find out how to apply for unemployment.

SEEK COUNSEL

You need people who will stand behind you, support you, and offer wisdom. If you don't have a mentor already, then it is time to get one. Your mentor could be a family friend or grandparent, a pastor or elder in your church, or someone at work. A mentor can help you sort through your questions and offer both encouragement and direction. Your mentor should be both someone you trust and someone who can give you objective feedback, not just tell you what you want to hear.

Chris, a thirty-year-old, says he has had two men in his life who have taken time to invest in him. "They have met with me and prayed with me and encouraged me more than I can begin to express," he says. "Without these men in my life I really doubt that I would be where I am now. They have traveled the roads that I am beginning to walk and are a wealth of knowledge."

Mentors can help you define what you want to do and provide insight as to what it will take to get there. They can help you focus on your goals, hold you accountable, and help chart a course for your future.

If you don't have a mentor, begin looking around at your work and church and among your neighbors and family. Do you have someone you look up to? Don't be afraid to ask someone to be a mentor; just be sure they know exactly what you are looking for. Define the terms of the relationship. How often will you meet and under what circumstances? For example, meeting for lunch once a month might work perfectly. Be clear about your needs. Do you want someone to bounce ideas off of or discuss career paths with? Are you looking for someone who will simply listen and pray? Let the mentor know your specific needs. And also include a time frame. You may want to suggest a trial period of three months to see if the mentoring relationship is working. If it is not or either of you is too busy, then there is a prearranged easy out.

DEVELOP A SUPPORT SYSTEM

In order to live a balanced life, you need to be in relationships with others. People you can trust are essential to living a healthy life. Not only will they encourage you when you are down, they will also hold you accountable to standards you set for yourself. They'll challenge you to make the best decisions with your time and resources. Your friends and family can provide support and opportunities to give to others as well as help you recognize what is truly important.

YOUR SUPPORT SYSTEM

You need people to be part of your support system. Reflect on the drawing below and write in the names of people who support you. Consider family members, friends, neighbors, coworkers, and mentors.

GET INVOLVED IN YOUR COMMUNITY

Don't let your life just be about your home and work. Look for opportunities to serve others. Become a part of activities and events taking place in your area. Volunteer at church, get involved in a civic group, join a mentoring program. Teach or take a class at a local college, even if you have a degree. When you invest in your local community, you naturally gain a sense of balance.

YOUR COMMUNITY

Part of being in a support system means supporting others. Reflect on the drawing below and write in the names of people you support, encourage, and strengthen on a regular basis. Consider family members, friends, neighbors, coworkers, and mentors.

TAKE A BREAK

Remember to take a Sabbath. Since the foundation of the world, God has been an advocate of downtime. A quick look at Genesis reminds us that even God took one day to rest. And if the never-tiring Creator of the universe takes five, how much more should you and I? The principle behind the Sabbath is rest. It's giving your mind, body, and spirit time to rejuvenate, reconnect with God, and relax.

The benefits of such downtime are priceless. Marcus, a twenty-eight-year-old full-time graduate student, says he is constantly struggling to balance the demands on his time. "Self care, I am learning, is extremely vital and often overlooked," he says. "When we take the time to be still and take inventory of what is going on not only in our lives but with our spirits, much is revealed. Out of that knowledge, we are able to discern the dry places and channel refreshment to those areas. We are then able to serve more effectively and joyfully. Although it is not rocket science, it is important to state that you simply can't give what you don't have."

Taking one day a week off doesn't come naturally for most people. It requires planning, saying no to extra activities, and guarding your time. But it's well worth the effort.

REMEMBER THE IMPORTANCE OF JOY

True joy embraces gratitude, excitement, and celebration. Joy is an inward celebration that isn't dependent on outward circumstances (though they sometimes help!). In the hustle and bustle of every day, it is easy to forget the important role that joy plays in your life. You may experience temporary happiness from acquiring new material goods, but joy isn't bound by stuff. True joy fills the innermost parts of your being.

Every so often it is important to take a step back and consider how you are living your life. When was the last time you felt truly joyful? Countless objects, items, and activities will bring you happiness: a delicious meal, a new outfit, a job promotion. But what brings you joy? Is it your relationships? the way you spend your free time? serving others? a sense of humor? Record your answer below.

_____

_____

_____

_____

_____

_____

Reflect on what changes you need to make to foster more joy in your life. What do you need to do in order to lead a more joyful life?

_____

_____

_____

_____

_____

_____

Three Hot Career Trends

Here are some of the hottest career trends as observed by the Herman Trend Alert (www.hermangroup.com):

• A report in *Strategic Business Futurists* revealed that twenty-four million Americans currently work in jobs that require nontraditional working hours (nights and evenings), and the number is likely to increase. This trend is in part due to global relationships, where people around the world are working in different time zones, and also to manufacturing facilities that want to use their machinery around the clock.

• An increasing number of companies are becoming partially or wholly virtual. Some companies do not even maintain headquarters offices. People work from their homes—across the country or around the world—connected by cell phones, voice-over-Internet protocol (VOiP), voice and video conference call systems, fax machines, and live video over the Internet. Some people never share the same physical location as their coworkers. The changes in work relationships will contribute to the development of a whole new set of skills for managers, as well as for nonmanagement employees.

• There is a growing trend toward the use of niche job boards among those seeking jobs. A recent study revealed that 78 percent of corporate employment specialists prefer niche sites. A variety of sites are available. Builders visit www.constructionjobs.com. Salespeople often use www.accountmanager.com, www.salesjobs.com, and www.marketingjobs.com. Computer-related jobs can be found at www.computerwork.com and www.dice.com. Senior executives can find job opportunities at www.netshare.com and www.execunet.com.

.0009

Movement:

What's Next?

Gosh.

Napoleon Dynamite

It all began with an innocent bowl of tortilla soup given to my husband as a thank-you for washing some hard-to-reach windows.

My six-foot-eight Norwegian giant had graciously offered to help a neighbor and returned home with a pint of made-from-scratch tortilla soup. It didn't just smell delicious; it tasted even better. The rich blend of tomatoes, peppers, chicken, and thin tortilla strips produced a slightly sweet but spicy savor. Small pieces of hominy added heartiness to the blend. After the second bite, I was filled with a sudden confidence and resolve.

I, too, could make tortilla soup.

I immediately opened my favorite cookbook—the Internet—and began surfing for the best recipe. Rather than settle on a single list of ingredients, I decided to cut and paste from those that sounded best and concoct my own artistic creation.

I headed to the store and purchased a can of hominy for the very first time in my life. Hominy is kind of like corn on steroids. It resembles corn-off-the-cob except for the jumbo shape and extra-starchy taste. It's available in both white and yellow, and it's usually located near the tacos and salsa in your local grocery.

The best thing about hominy beyond its presence in torti-lla soup is actually saying the word. *Hominy. Hominy. Hominy.* It just rolls off the tongue like a blend of *harmony* and *homily,* except that you can eat it! Yum.

Well, my first attempt at tortilla soup was a success except for one little factor: I decided not to remove the seeds—where all the heat is located—from the jalapeño. The result was man-on-fire tortilla soup that left everyone sweating at the end of the meal. But I was committed to the process, and before you could say "Pepe Gonzales," I was on a full-fledged tortilla-soup kick. I decided to make a second batch of soup before we had even finished the first.

When I returned to the grocery store, I noticed the large cans of hominy on sale. For only forty cents more I could bring home an industrial-size can of hominy. I couldn't resist the temptation. So I left the innocent one-pound-thirteen-ounce can of hominy on the shelf and selected the six-pound-twelve-ounce can. Yep. You read that right. Six pounds of hominy. I knew my husband was going to kill me. But what the heck.

I made a second batch of tortilla soup with seedless jalapeños, and it turned out delicious. I still had five pounds of hominy left! What to do?

Why not experiment?

I tried using hominy in chili, and it turned out well. I discov-ered the hominy was firm enough to hold together in the chili without breaking down. With two pounds of hominy remain-ing, I decided to try another experiment: hominy chicken soup. It turned out bad—*really* bad. When you place hominy in a mild-flavored soup, it overpowers everything so the entire soup tastes like hominy. Yuck. Solution: Add tomatoes, jalapeños, green chilies, and tortilla strips and transform chicken soup into tortilla soup. Whala! My freezer is now over-flowing with hominy flavored soups and chili—for better or worse, depending on your perspective and taste buds.

My husband made me promise never to buy anything industrial-sized, especially if the label says *hominy,* ever again. And I did—with two fingers crossed behind my back.

I wish this story were purely fiction, but it's real life, and humbly, it's my life. This is the crazy blend of exploring and experimenting and succeeding and failing and flailing and making the ridiculous come alive that gives life meaning and direction and flavor, even with its mysterious blend of trial and error.

It's interesting how this whole hominy-filled tale began with an innocent bowl of tortilla soup from a neighbor. There's just no telling what single event or encounter will send you off in a whole new direction.

If you're still wondering, *What the heck am I going to do with my life?* then know that you are not alone. Some people consider life one big adventure, but if you break it down life is really a collection of little paths and journeys met with surprising side trails, sudden roadblocks, wondrous overlooks, and beau-tiful vistas.

> You were designed for movement. You were meant to live a verb-filled life.

Consider the great commission of Matthew 28. What does Jesus tell his followers?

Go.

Make.

Teach.

He concludes with one small but significant, verb-filled, powerful promise:

Be sure.

Of what? you may wonder.

"Be sure of this: I am with you always, even to the end of the age" (Matthew 28:20, NLT).

Notice that Jesus doesn't give a minute-by-minute breakdown of everything you're supposed to do—potty breaks included. He simply sends you in a direction: upward and outward. Along the way, he promises to be with you, even when you're not quite sure where you are or what that next step is supposed to be.

Your next step may be as simple as filling out and sending in an application. It may be talking to a family member about a possible job. It may be packing up and moving like you've been secretly wanting to for several years.

It is never too late to make a course change. It's never too late to pursue your passion. You can go back to school, launch a new business, or change professions. You may have to enroll online or build your business one day at a time, but you can make a change.

The Bible is filled with people of passion and people of movement. Sarah and Abraham became parents. Noah built an ark. David went from shepherd boy to king. Peter went from fisherman to evangelist. Paul went from church persecutor to church builder. Along the way, these men and women had many of the same self-doubts, fears, and questions that you and I have today. Yet God accomplished much through their lives.

How much more will he accomplish through yours?

Just because you don't know what God wants you to do tomorrow doesn't mean you don't know what he wants you to do today.

So go ahead.

Be brave.

Apply.

Start something new.

You never know what kind of opportunities and innovations might be around the next corner.

To Artists Everywhere:

I am not an artist, merely a wannabe of sorts. While I paint with words, sculpt ideas, and do my best to carve images into the human mind, I spend my free time standing in awe of your creations. Your work. Your art. With every glimpse, I marvel not just at your creativity but also the sacrifices you have made to create such beautiful art. Throughout history, being an artist has never been easy. Not then. Not now.

Our journeys are different but in many ways the same. We are doing our best to pursue our passion . . . to develop the talents, gifts, and longings that have been in our souls from the beginning. And it isn't easy.

I have had to learn most of my lessons the hard way. For instance, the fruit of living out my passion comes in seasons. Naively, I thought I would have a moment when all my work was rewarded by the impact it made on people's lives. Yet I've discovered that the fruit—the real life-impacting nature of what I do—doesn't come every season. It doesn't even come every year. Without a doubt, I feel called to write. It's something I'm passionate about, and I feel truly alive when I do it.

The high moments of following your calling and passion may be fewer than you think, but when you do experience them, they somehow manage to make the entire journey worthwhile. When you are a writer, there's nothing like receiving a letter, e-mail, or note from a reader that says your work breathed life into their soul. I have had the privilege of working on such projects, and I always save the letters in a folder near my desk. I reread the notes and messages when creative times are nonexistent.

I've also learned that pursuing your passion is going to take longer than you expect, cost more than you think, and require you to grow in ways you never imagined. Writing has been a long, challenging journey for me. For the first seven years, I always worked a second or third job in order to make ends meet. At one point, I was working three additional jobs in order to survive. One night I turned over in bed and felt extreme pain on the left side of my lower back. It turns out that the compounded stress had taken its toll on my back muscles: Several ribs were dislocated from my spine. I'll never forget the doctor's words: "Your body is trying to talk to you. It is saying that you are doing too much. If you don't make a change, then your body is going to speak louder next time."

I'm a slow learner, but I finally dropped one of the jobs and began taking better care of myself. Pursuing your passion is challenging, exhausting, and intense, but it is also joyful, rewarding, and satisfies something inside of you that nothing else will. It has been said that when you minister in a manner consistent with the personality, talents, life experiences, and gifts God gave you, you experience fulfillment, satisfaction, and fruitfulness. Anyone who has ever stepped out in faith to fulfill their calling knows the depth of this truth. Pursuing your passion and calling will cost you, but as you already know, the rewards are incredible.

I've also discovered the importance of reminding myself of God's faithfulness. When you respond to the passion and calling God has placed in your life, you are going to experience breaking points. You will find yourself in situations that test your stamina, strength, integrity, patience, and ability. On more occasions than I care to remember, I've found myself wondering, Is God really going to come through this time? He may have come through a hundred times before, but I can't help but ask the question again. At those moments, it is good to have a record of God's faithfulness.

In the Old Testament, people built altars as places of remembrance. The rock structures served as memorials of moments when God proved himself true. In modern times, we also need to keep a record. It may be something as simple as a journal or blog. Reflecting on God's faithfulness is not only an act of worship; it helps strengthen our faith for the situations we face again and again.

One of my biggest struggles as an artist wannabe has been staying focused on doing what God has uniquely called me to do. It is so easy to get distracted from God's calling. By looking at what others have accomplished,

I can dream myself into doing a hundred different projects, but I'm slowly discovering the importance of remaining focused on what God has called me to do. In my writing, I have stuck with nonfiction. I have had editors and fellow writers ask me to consider writing fiction, but it just isn't something I feel compelled to do right now. Maybe one day I will develop plots and storylines, but for now I am content. Besides, I figure that what really happens to people is far more bizarre than what people can imagine and put on paper.

So my wish, my prayer, and my dream for you is that you continue to pursue the passion God has placed on your heart. I want you to create and design images, artwork, and structures that this world has never seen. My hope is that the God-infused ideas and thoughts and prayers that haunt your soul would become a reality as you step out in faith to do what you were created to do. And that in the end, you would be able to look at your work confidently and humbly in awe of what has been done through you. My prayers are with you.

One of your biggest fans,
Margaret

Discussion Questions

.0001 **Launch:** Where Do We Go from Here?

1. When you were a child, what did you dream of doing when you grew up? In what ways are those dreams still alive in you today? How have they changed? How have *you* changed?

2. In what ways has your life unfolded as you expected? What has surprised you most about your life? How have you responded to those surprises?

3. Can you relate to the question *What the heck am I going to do with my life?* On a scale of 1 to 10, how much are you currently wrestling with that question? On a scale of 1 to 10, how much do you see yourself wrestling with it in the next five years?

4. In what ways does the question of what you're going to do with your life go deeper than just a profession or job?

.0002 **Direction:** What Pushes You?

1. What are your family's expectations about your career? your relationships? your future? How have their expectations affected your choices? Which of their expectations have you met? In which areas have you done something different? What has been the result?

2. Describe a time when you were asked to meet a need. How did you respond? Looking back, do you think you were called to meet that need? Describe what it feels like for you to really help someone.

3. Do you tend to ask God for help more in little situations (like lost keys) or in big situations? What prevents you from asking for his help more often?

4. In what ways have you experienced God speaking to you? Describe a specific situation in which you felt God using Scripture, circumstance, or someone else to speak into your life. How did you respond? Have you ever felt God speak to you but decided to ignore him? What was the result?

5. What factors have pushed you in deciding what you're going to do with your life? Which of these have been positive influences? Which have been negative? Where do you go when you need advice and direction in life?

.0003 **Calling:** What Pulls You?

1. How have you heard the word *calling* used? What do you understand it to mean? How have these definitions shaped your view of what *your* calling is?

2. Do you believe (consciously or subconsciously) that some callings have more value than others? What impact does this

have on your feelings about what you are going to do with your life?

3. Do you believe in destiny? What does it mean to you? What role does God play in your understanding of destiny?

4. Think of a person from the Bible who responded to their calling. What was the result? What were the high and low points of their life?

.0004 **Passion:** What Makes You Fly Inside?

1. If you could do anything with your life, assuming that time and money were no object, what would you choose to do? What's stopping you?

2. Have you talked about your passion with others? What was their reaction? How did their responses make you feel about your passion?

3. How do you respond to people who are sharing their passions with you? Are there any changes you need to make in your responses?

4. What are some of the practical barriers to pursuing your passion? Money? Fear? Discouragement? Uncertainty? Something else? What can you do to overcome these obstacles?

5. Describe a time when you took a risk. What was the result? What did you learn? Looking back, would you do anything differently if faced with the same situation?

.0005 Innovation: Where Does It Begin?

1. Describe a time when you were an innovator (in your family, church, workplace, etc.). How did your unique personality, passion, and experiences prepare you for that situation?

2. What do you think is the most difficult part of being an innovator? What is the most rewarding?

3. Have you seen any moments of innovation in your community, workplace, church, or school? How have they impacted you? Were you inspired? discouraged? envious? Why?

4. What list of *buts* do you give when God calls you to do something new? What do you think God's response is? How can you get past any objections or fears?

.0006 Reality: Why Is This So Hard?

1. What role does your faith play when dealing with the realities of your job? of your life?

2. Have you ever had a job you hated? What was so difficult about the job? What were the personal costs of staying there? What did the experience teach you about yourself?

3. What expectations do you have about your career? Where do you think these expectations or assumptions came from? How has your (or others') experience changed them?

4. Have you ever had one door of opportunity open just as another shut? Have you had to make a tough decision between career paths or areas of study? What was the result? Do you ever regret or second-guess any of your decisions?

.0007 **Impact:** Will It Live beyond You?

1. When have you witnessed a simple act of kindness? When have you performed one? What impact did both have on you?

2. How can you make a difference in your workplace? In what ways do you see your job as a place to reflect Christ? How does looking at your job this way change your perspective?

3. How do the principles of compassion and integrity factor in when you think about making a difference? What other principles come to mind?

4. Describe a moment when your work and personal values collided. How did you respond? What was the final outcome?

.0008 **Balance:** Can You Hold It All Together?

1. Make a list of five adjectives that describe you. What defines you as a person? In what ways is it tempting to allow what you do to define who you are?

2. In what areas of life do you tend to overcommit? What types of situations or opportunities are the hardest for you to say no to? What are some things you could say yes to if your time was more balanced?

3. Describe your perfect work environment.
Would you choose a quiet desk job? actively working with other people? a fast-paced or more laid-back environment? Are there any changes in your current workplace that you can make to create a healthier environment for you?

4. Have you ever had a mentor? What impact did that person have on your life? Have you been a mentor to someone else? How did that experience affect you? If you haven't been a mentor, what is stopping you?

5. Do you take a Sabbath? What does it look like in your life? How does it affect the rest of your week? How can you adjust your schedule to make room for a day of rest?

.0009 **Movement:** What's Next?

1. In what ways are you currently pursuing your passion?

2. What is the next practical step in pursuing your passion?

3. What is stopping you from taking the next step to do the very thing you feel called and created to do?

What the heck are you going to do with your life? Continue the discussion online at www.margaretfeinberg.blogspot.com.

Notes

.0000 Spark: Introductions

1. The tests in this book are not scientifically validated, but they are meant to be valuable resources for self-reflection and assessment.

.0001 Launch: Where Do We Go from Here?

1. People have asked me what I mean by "not missions material." My time in Honduras was one of those everything-that-could-go-wrong-did experiences. I was ill most of the time and unable to do any of the "missions" work because of a broken vehicle. Halfway through the time, I was robbed at knifepoint and lost everything but my passport and a few dollars. I remember talking to several sets of missionaries who had been in the area for twenty-plus years. When I shared my story, I asked, "Is this normal?" They looked at me as if I were from Mars. They couldn't relate to my story in the least. At that point, I knew I was not cut out for the mission field. That was a tough realization because I always thought that the people who really loved God served overseas. That's how it had been portrayed in church while I was growing up. It has taken me years to understand that everyone is created for a different purpose, and no matter the job or country, we're all called to serve others.

.0002 Direction: What Pushes You?

1. Jerry Slocum interview by the author, December 15, 2004.

2. I opted for a Norwegian.

3. ABC, Inc., *Life of Luxury*, http://abc.go.com/specials/lifeofluxury.html/.

4. Thomas J. Stanley, PhD and William D. Danko, PhD, *The Millionaire Next Door* (New York: MFJ Books, 2002).

5. Lance Armstrong with Sally Jenkins, *It's Not about the Bike: My Journey Back to Life* (New York: Berkley Books, 2001), 4.

6. Adapted from Lawrence A. Stuenkel, *From Here to There: A Self-Paced Program for Transition in Employment*, 5th ed. (Tempe, Ariz.: Facts on Demand Press, 2002), 50. Used with permission.

7. CBS Worldwide, Inc., "Alice Coles of Bayview," http://www.cbsnews.com/stories/2003/11/6/60minutes/main585793.shtml; Zanetta Doyle, "Community Thwarts Building of Prison," National Association of Development Organizations, http://www.nado.org/pubs/dj032.html; United States Department of Agriculture, "Success Stories: Rural Development Helps Revitalize One of Virginia's Poorest and Historically Underserved Communities," http://www.rurdev.usda.gov/rd/stories/va-bayview.html.

8. The topic of recognizing God's voice is examined more thoroughly in *God Whispers: Learning to Hear His Voice* (Relevant Books, 2002).

.0003 Calling: What Pulls You?

1. Ken Frantz interview by the author, December 24, 2004.

2. John Piper, *Don't Waste Your Life* (Wheaton, Ill.: Crossway, 2003), 31.

3. Os Hillman interview by the author, December 23, 2004. For more information on work and faith ministries visit www.marketplaceleaders.org and www.faithandworkresources.com/.

.0004 Passion: What Makes You Fly Inside?

1. Bill Stoffregen interview by the author, December 23, 2004.

2. Anne Abernathy interview by the author, December 22, 2004.

.0005 Innovation: Where Does It Begin?

1. Keith Gibson interview by the author, 2005.

2. *Merriam-Webster's Collegiate Dictionary,* 11th ed., s.v. "Innovation."

3. The Gleitsman Foundation, "Award of Achievement Honorees," http://www.gleitsman.org/achievement.html/.

.0006 Reality: Why Is This So Hard?

1. Dois I. Rosser Jr. interview by the author, December 22, 2004.

2. NBC.com, "Michael Jordan," http://www.nba.com/playerfile/michael_jordan/index.html/.

3. Based on a study in *Organizational Behavior: Managing People and Organizations* by Gregory Moorhead and Ricky W. Griffin (New York: Houghton Mifflin, 2004), 50.

4. Betsy Taylor interview by the author, January 17, 2005.

.0007 Impact—Will It Live beyond You?

1. Bob Buford, *Halftime: Changing Your Game Plan from Success to Significance* (Grand Rapids, Mich.: Zondervan, 1994), 30, 160.

2. Brian Mosley interview by the author, January 12, 2005.

3. Betsy Taylor interview by the author, January 17, 2005.

4. Dennis W. Bakke, *Joy at Work: A Revolutionary Approach to Fun on the Job* (Seattle, Wash.: PVG, 2005), 25.

.0008 Balance: Can You Hold It All Together?

1. Rene Rodriguez, "Movies," *The Miami Herald,* http://ae.miami.com/entertainment/ui/miami/movie.html?id=175785&reviewId=16563&startDate=01/13/2005&1c/.

About the Author

Margaret Feinberg spent the year after college traveling, working multiple part-time jobs, and wondering *What the heck am I going to do with my life?* She finally decided that if she could do anything, she really wanted to write. So she sent query letters off to several magazines. Eight years and some eight hundred magazine articles later, she says she has found her passion and calling.

Margaret has written or contributed to more than twenty books, including *Twentysomething: Surviving and Thriving in the Real World* (W Publishing, 2004), which takes a compelling look at the biggest issues facing today's twenties and is based on more than one hundred interviews with pastors, counselors, and researchers, as well as twentysomethings from across the country. The book helps readers sort through questions including Who am I? What's my purpose? Will anyone ever love me? and Why is no one clapping?

Some of her other titles include *Just Married: What Might Surprise You about the First Few Years of Marriage, How to Be a Grown-Up: 247 Lab-Tested Strategies for Conquering Your World* (coauthored with her husband), and *God Whispers: Learning to Hear His Voice.*

Margaret and her husband, Leif, live in Juneau, Alaska, where she loves hiking, kayaking, and chasing the northern lights. During the long dark winters, she's been known to become addicted to reruns of *Law & Order, CSI,* and anything related to reality television. She dreams of traveling to Prince

Edward Island (where *Anne of Green Gables* was filmed), eating pancakes with fresh maple syrup in Vermont, searching for hobbits in New Zealand, and exploring China. She loves lazy afternoons filled with great books, warm down comforters, Splenda-sweetened flavored coffee, and mangoes.

To contact Margaret Feinberg online, visit her Web site at www.margaretfeinberg.com or e-mail her at margaret@margaretfeinberg.com.

Send snail mail to:

Margaret Feinberg

PO Box 32953

Juneau, AK 99803

The classics.

Love 'em,

hate 'em,

avoid 'em like the plague.

Most of us fit into one of these categories when it comes to stuff written a long time ago in lands far, far away by people named St. Augustine, St. Teresa, or Brother Lawrence.

But you'd be surprised at how similar their questions and struggles are to what we're dealing with today. Just like us, they loved, doubted, failed, and grew. And in the midst of all of it, they took a chance on following God and were absolutely blown away by the results!

Now it's your turn to be blown away. This book contains the revolutionary ideas of twenty of the most influential Christian thinkers and writers of all time. And their messages are as relevant today as they were decades and, in some cases, centuries ago.

Yep. These are definitely twenty of our favorites. Hopefully they'll become some of yours as well.

Pick up your copy of *Twenty Things You Should Read* at a bookstore near you!

Releases June 2006